Beyond Brexit: The Blueprint

In memory of
Ronald Banks

Fred Harrison's previous publications include

As Evil Does (2015)
The Traumatised Society (2012)
Ricardo's Law (2006)
Boom Bust (2005)
Power in the Land (1983)

Fred Harrison's blogs are on
www.sharetherents.org

His videos are on
www.youtube.com/user/geophilos

Twitter: **@geophilos**

Beyond Brexit:
The Blueprint

Land
Research
Trust

First published in 2016 by
Land Research Trust
7 Kings Road
Teddington
TW11 OQB, UK

British Library Cataloguing in Publication Data
A catalogue record of this book is available
from the British Library

ISBN 978-0-9956351-0-4

Designed by Ian Kirkwood design
www.ik-design.co.uk

Printed by IngramSpark

Contents

Beyond Brexit: The Blueprint

Fred Harrison

The United Kingdom needs a new doctrine of statecraft: one that aligns fiscal honesty with the acceptance that human rights come with personal responsibilities. This would yield a partnership between people and government, launching a renaissance that would serve as the beacon of hope for the nations of Europe.

The European Union's leaders know they are confronted by an existential crisis. But they deceive themselves with the idea that the UK needs the EU more than the EU needs the UK. That false belief is intended to place Prime Minister Theresa May's government at a disadvantage in the discussions over Brexit. The EU needs a close association with Britain for many reasons, and the bargaining chips are stacked in the UK's favour. The UK's ace is the freedom, post-Brexit, to expand her home market by more than what would be lost if the EU raised tariff barriers against British exports. *But to create that expanded market, the people must mandate Parliament to undertake the reform of taxation to achieve Mrs May's social agenda:*

- *eliminate the inequalities that shame Britain*
- *restore growth and share benefits in an inclusive economy; and*
- *confront the scandal of premature deaths among low income families.*

Reforms must also plug the gap in the human rights doctrine: rights must be matched with responsibilities. And trade deals with the rest of the world must be based on mutually beneficial terms.

Mrs May's mission depends on her government's ability to dismantle the tax barriers that deprive Britain of about £493bn every year. Which is the additional wealth and welfare that the population would produce if revenue was raised in ways that enhanced personal freedoms and social cohesion. Hints of those reforms appeared in a Financial Times *editorial (July 20, 2016): "Identify ways to deliver a swifter boost to the economy, such as cuts in consumption tax, incentives for investment, or changes in land taxes that would spur development".*

Prologue

B *eyond Brexit* identifies the errors of the political and economic philosophies which bedevilled the 20th century, and as a Blueprint it seeks to help Europe re-route itself from a dead-end journey.

The nations of Europe failed to make a full recovery from the traumas they faced as far back as 1918. The continent is now reliving the dilemmas it faced at the end of the First World War. Back then, with the blood-letting over, the architecture of a new political order had to be envisaged. The statesmen who converged on Paris to work out the blueprint carried a heavy responsibility. Four empires had folded: the German, Austro-Hungarian, Russian and Ottoman. A new settlement was needed to fill the geo-political void, so that the new nation-states could become peaceful partners. One man stood out against the crowd – John Maynard Keynes.

Britain's emissary to the Peace Conference listened, and grew fearful by the day. The diplomats were making a mess of their project, and he refused to be party to the final outcome. He resigned his commission three weeks before the Treaty of Versailles was signed, and he returned to Cambridge to write *The Economic Consequences of the Peace.*

His instincts about the treaty were soundly based, but his assessment of the economic events that had prevailed over the previous 50 years was faulty. As a direct consequence, Keynes was to play a part in misdirecting the future of Europe.

Today, Europe's leaders are no better informed on the terms that would secure peace and prosperity. Three of them – from Germany, France and Italy – helicoptered onto the Italian island of Ventotene on 22 August, 2016, to affirm their faith in the European project. But the European Union is re-running the policy errors of the 1930s. And Keynesianism is part of the problem.

The crises in both the UK and in Europe stem from a failure of governance. The context was set out by Keynes in his critique of the Paris Peace treaty. He sought to explain the economic, demographic and philosophical trends which led up to the first world war in terms of the nature of power in capitalism. His flawed analysis serves as one point of departure for scoping out a new blueprint to serve a dual purpose: meet the aspirations of all Europeans, and empower the UK Government to arrive at a mutually beneficial settlement with the remaining 27 members of the European Union.

Keynes erred in viewing as beneficial the inequality which afflicted Europe at the end of the 19th century. He argued that, without the unequal distribution of the fabulous resources that were being generated by the industrial nations, it would not have been possible to save and invest in infrastructure. The railways, in particular, were vital to open up the bread baskets of America. Europe's growing population had relied on the New World for food, and capitalism -- because of the privileged accumulation of wealth by people who chose not to consume their riches – made it possible to fund the expansion that fed the growing populations.

' I seek only to point out that the principle of accumulation based on inequality was a vital part of the pre-war order of Society and of progress as we then understood it, and to emphasise that this principle depended on unstable psychological conditions, which it may be impossible to re-create.'[1]

The "unstable psychological conditions" were preserved, and Keynes contributed to their preservation by suggesting how to sustain capitalism and its unequal distribution of resources.

Keynes insisted that, to fund infrastructure such as railway networks, it was necessary to allow the "profits" from the economy to flow into the hands of capitalists. This was a crude rationalisation of the way income was distributed. He disregarded the nuanced classical doctrines that originated in the 18th century, which were fleshed out by a few philosophers (like John Stuart Mill) in the 19th century. Furthermore, by the time he came to pen his critique in 1919, he had at his disposal the rigorous theorising of one of his contemporaries in Cambridge. Alfred Marshall had analysed the optimum arrangements for funding what we now call "public goods", and he showed that infrastructure needed to be funded out of economic rents. In other words, if governance had been based on the fiscal system commended by Adam Smith, a public/private partnership would have emerged in the 19th century to drive social evolution to a new level of inclusive prosperity.

▶ The costs of public infrastructure would have been funded out of the nation's land rents, the stream of value that everyone helped to create.

▶ The formation of the new capital required by private enterprises in the rapidly expanding economy would have been funded by consumers.

This prospectus was well attested in the economic literature available to Keynes. To tap the new riches that would be delivered by this partnership, however, the power brokers needed the moral sensibilities that had led Adam Smith to commend the net income of the economy as the State's appropriate source of revenue. That net income, he wrote, was the annual ground rent (AGR). The social need for such a fiscal reform was manifest in the destitution of

---

1 John Maynard Keynes (1920), *The Economic Consequences of the Peace*, London: Labour Research Department, p.19.

the working population. Social tensions emerged in disputes over who owned the benefits which flowed from the services provided by nature and society.

Keynes would have none of it. He was emphatic that "the land question" had been solved. So his analysis of the cyclical booms and busts of the capitalist economy diverted attention from the one structural flaw that caused the socially-significant crises. He put in its place a monetary remedy that continues to entrance governments to this day.

The decision taken by the people of the United Kingdom on Thursday 23 June, 2016, to leave the European Union, was a reaction to a visibly intolerable state of affairs. That decision need not be a disaster for anyone, but the reaction of despair by those who opposed Brexit was understandable. They could not visualise how to renegotiate a new future that would enhance the lives of populations in both the UK and the EU. Their fear of existential threats – like Keynes in the earlier age – was well grounded. But the analysts on whom they relied for informed guidance failed to accurately diagnose the causes of the trends that led the majority to cast their vote in favour of Brexit. Without sound diagnosis, there is (once again) little prospect of reconstituting Europe's nations on durable foundations.

Back in the 1950s, the social scientists who advised governments should have alerted the founding fathers of the European project that a free trade area, by itself, would trigger the re-emergence of a pan-European layer of exploitation.

▶ Under prevailing laws and institutions, Europe would be divided into a rich core and an impoverished periphery.

▶ Common policies – movement of people, a shared currency – would reinforce the privileges of the growth centres.

▶ The spatial periphery would become increasingly dependent on financial hand-outs from the bureaucratised centre.

▶ Institutionalised deprivation would turn millions of people into hostages: the status of Greece today.

A financial algorithm for untangling this tragedy exists. It is the formula that made civilisation possible. It is now wilfully ostracised by academia. But the knowledge will not go away. It has the power to heal the divisions which afflict Europe. It entails the setting of pan-European governance on principles that would rebalance the relationships between nations. But to achieve this outcome, statesmen and social scientists need to muster the moral courage to rethink the reasons why Europe embarked on a course for tragedy. And the four nations of the UK need to participate in that project by charting a new course into the future for Britain.

The 1st Law of Governance

Governments are supposed to administer the State on terms that deliver stability. People tend to ask for little more than a set of rules which they can take for granted, so that they can go about the business of meeting their daily needs. This is so, whether society operates on the principles of monarchy, aristocracy or democracy. The implicit social contract is not fulfilled when people whose hands are on the levers of power fail to comply with the 1st Law of Governance: deliver stability and security for everyone in the realm. When that law is flouted, the welfare of some sections of the population is sacrificed to advance the privileged interests of what tends to be a minority of the population. The outcome is social fragmentation and, when the ruptures become too painful, the prospect of civil war.

For five millennia, nation-state governance was based on the capacity to protect a territory, collect the rent and provide the population with the services that secured their allegiance. Public finance was at the heart of the organising mechanism for administering power. The character of power and the prosperity of the people were determined by the extent to which the 1st Law of Governance was observed.

- Society was at peace when revenue was collected out of the *net income* that people generated. This was the value that remained after people had deducted their wages and the costs of the capital they invested in production.

- Civil strife became a risk when the net income was misappropriated (privatised). For, as a consequence, this meant that people's wages had to be taxed to fund the State.

- Fiscal misgovernance led to sovereign indebtedness, which transferred the costs of today's services onto the labour of future generations.

Dysfunctional forms of taxation are ultimately responsible for the stresses (like poverty) that divide families, communities and nations.

Net income — technically called *economic rent* — is the most sensitive barometer of a nation's wealth and welfare. Good governance adds to net income; bad forms of governance subtract from the total. And so, to measure the performance of the people in power, the best gauge is the total of rent produced. Taxes that damage people's wealth and welfare necessarily reduce the amount of rent that they can produce to fund the myriad forms of culture that constitute a civilised society.

The distance between governance and the needs of the people can be stretched to breaking point. Italy is a classic case of how the political class has lost its capacity to govern. Indicators of disempowerment were derived by the International Monetary Fund from both the public and private sectors.

This led the IMF to conclude, in July 2016, that Italy had embarked on "two lost decades". Clues were to be found in the

- **high taxes:** the costs of an "inefficient public sector", and civil service wage growth, exceeded the gains in productivity, and had contributed to the crash in productivity. And

- **brain drain:** educated Italians were driven abroad because they could not find work at home. The despair was registered in the rate of youth unemployment, which exceeded 35%.

Misgovernance in Italy long predated 2008. It is based on two social fault lines — in politics and economics — which follow the contours of the two geological fault lines that render the country vulnerable to seismic shocks. The IMF tracked the political shocks in a report published in July 2016. Italy's banks were bankrupt, governments were distracted by corruption scandals, and policy-makers were not in the business of restoring integrity to their administrations. Politicians do not regard rules as sacrosanct: they are meant to be bent. The government of Mateo Renzi, for example, wanted the EU to bend its rules so that its banks could be bailed out, with the cost imposed on taxpayers rather than bank shareholders.

The economic shocks, such as the "bad debts", were concentrated in southern regions and anchored in the sectors — construction and furniture manufacturers — that were hostage to the fortunes of land speculation. Real estate speculation was institutionalised: sanctioned by successive governments through their choice of tax policies.

The two social fault lines collided in the earthquake in August 2016. Whole villages in the mountains collapsed, nearly 300 people died and 3,000 were rendered homeless. Many of the buildings were illegally constructed; and there was a strong suspicion that the builders had flouted regulations by using more sand than cement to hold the bricks together.

The Italian mafia exercises extensive control over the construction industry. This enables them to extract part of the nation's rents via influence over politicians and the contracts for the construction of highways and public buildings. Italy's anti-mafia agency has started an investigation into how recently constructed buildings like schools collapsed like packs of cards.

Misgovernance is responsible for Italy's North/South divide and the ability of lawless agents to ransack the public purse. Civic irresponsibility reflects political irresponsibility. But the IMF failed to offer advice on how to re-base governance on the principles of honesty and integrity. Instead, it offered platitudes: "less distortive taxation, including broadening the tax base and introducing a modern real estate tax".[1] This policy combination helped to drive countries such as Spain and Ireland into the financial buffers of 2008.

But one economist has discerned a crumb of comfort. Public spending prompted by the earthquake may more than offset the negative costs, resulting in a positive effect on the rate of GDP growth.[2]

---

1 IMF Executive Board 2016 Article IV Consultation with Italy, July 12, 2016. Press Release No. 16/329. http://www.imf.org/external/np/sec/pr/2016/pr16329.htm
2 Rachel Sanderson (2016), "Despair gives way to anger as Italy mourns", *Financial Times*, August 31.

1

Mrs May's Mission Impossible?

ON July 13, 2016, David Cameron resigned and Theresa May moved into No. 10 Downing Street. Her mission: withdraw the UK from the European Union and build an inclusive society. The economy would work for everyone. Mrs May's determination was driven by the knowledge that "right now, if you're born poor, you will die on average nine years earlier than others". Under her administration, employees would acquire the right of representation on the boards of the big companies where they worked; shareholders would have more say on the remuneration of corporate bosses, the housing crisis would be addressed, and there would be action over the gap between rich and poor. But without the tools to achieve her goals, Mrs May embarked on a course that would end in failure.

The new Prime Minister was sincere in her intentions, but she will be defeated by a form of governance that rests on a programmed-to-fail model of High Finance. The ideas and information that course through the digital super-highways are designed to deceive. They lure well-intentioned law-makers into promises they cannot keep. This process of misgovernance is a tragedy for everybody. Politicians are left frustrated by their inability to keep faith with the people who put them in power. And people at large are frustrated by a deep sense of betrayal. One outcome was the refusal by the majority who voted in the EU referendum to believe the experts who claimed that sovereign independence would be a disaster.

Politics, and the economy, operate within the confines of a fiscal model that prescribes the limits of what governments can achieve. And so, Mrs May walked into the biggest trap of all when she scoped out her plans on taxation.

' And tax. We need to talk about tax [*she insisted*]. Because we're Conservatives, and of course we believe in a low-tax economy, in which British businesses are more competitive and families get to keep more of what they earn – but we also understand that tax is the price we pay for living in a civilised society. No individual and no business, however rich, has succeeded all on their own. Their goods are transported by road, their workers are educated in schools, their customers are part of sophisticated networks taking in the private sector, the public sector and charities. It doesn't matter to me whether you're Amazon, Google or Starbucks, you have a duty to put something back, you have a debt to your fellow citizens, you have a responsibility to pay your taxes. So as Prime Minister, I will crack down on individual and corporate tax avoidance and evasion.

That statement was literally Churchillian in its significance. But the element missing from the statement was Churchill's solution to the problems highlighted by Mrs May: the need to reform the tax system itself. He understood that the damage caused by taxation is camouflaged by the authorised discourse on public finance. Mrs May needed to know that

▶ reducing tax rates intensifies problems like unaffordable house prices and divided communities;

▶ funding infrastructure like transport is biased to favour London and prejudice regional incomes; and

▶ cracking down on tax dodgers encourages corporations to devise alternative anti-social strategies.

The cause of these unintended outcomes is a land-and-tax legacy which privileges one section of society with unearned income, and its consequent impact on property prices, while penalising everyone with burdens that reduce productivity and the quality of their lives. A centripetal force prevails within the economy which overwhelms the palliative defences erected by politicians. That land-and-tax model incubates the deadly financial virus that weakens the capacity of people to achieve their economic and social potential. It is the malevolent mechanism which defeats the good intentions of decent politicians like Theresa May.

The antidote exists. If the May Government really wants to rebalance British society, to secure equal opportunity for everyone by addressing the "difficult truth", as she called it, she will have to rebalance the public's finances.

▶ Under the current land-and-tax model, the UK foregoes value of nearly £500 billion a year. This loss is caused by Treadmill Taxes like the EU's mandatory Value Added Tax (VAT).

To escape the clutches of this model of public finance, it is necessary to understand that tax policy is the foremost determinant of

1. how national income is allocated between the public and private sectors;

2. the power allocated to the owners of land, labour and capital; and

3. the quality of the relationships that prevail between the producing agents.

The fiscal paradigm ultimately determines the extent of personal freedom and social cohesion; and it shapes the capacity of society to meet its challenges and contribute to the welfare of future generations.

Mrs May's goals can be accomplished. The post-Brexit blueprint demonstrates how to rebalance the economy by placing the fiscal system on foundations that would deliver the most ambitious of outcomes, liberating people's aspirations by eradicating artificial constraints. But without the appropriate fiscal reforms,

---

Box 1:1 **Theresa May confronts "difficult truths"**

In commissioning a social audit to reveal the scale of inequalities in Britain's schools, universities, hospitals and the criminal justice system, the Prime Minister declared:

' *It will highlight the differences in outcomes for people of different backgrounds, in every area from health to education, childcare to welfare, employment, skills and criminal justice. This audit will reveal difficult truths, but we should not be apologetic about shining a light on injustices as never before. It is only by doing so we can make this country work for everyone, not just a privileged few.'* *

If the enquiry fails to address the role of governance in the discrimination that systematically disunites the kingdom, its assessments will not arrive at the appropriate remedies. Mrs May understands that spending power – the ability to buy houses near the best schools – was "selection by house prices". But creating grammar schools, by themselves, does not overcome the institutionalised discrimination which include the cultural constraints that are bred into the ghettoes of deprivation. Seaside towns, for example, are "dumping grounds" for social problems; grammar schools – as the evidence from the four decades after World War 2 indicates – did not erase the disadvantages of growing up in deprived districts.

* https://www.gov.uk/government/news/prime-minister-orders-government-audit-to-tackle-racial-disparities-in-public-service-outcomes

---

Mrs May's government will perpetuate the inequalities that are embedded in society (see Box 1:1). And that brings us to the Prime Minister's first embarrassing political problem, one that she has created for herself. Lawyers and accountants who peddle tax-avoidance schemes are to be held accountable. The taxman will go after the backroom schemers, not just the tax-dodgers, with fines equivalent to the revenue lost by HM Customs & Revenue. Mrs May's initiative was welcomed by the *Financial Times*: "May flexes her muscles over tax avoidance" (August 18, 2016). People who deprive the nation of its revenue will pay the price for their anti-social behaviour.

But the "rule of law" doctrine requires consistency: what is good for the goose is good for the gander. So Mrs May, if she retains the use of those taxes which deprive the public of £493bn every year, will be held responsible for short-changing the public purse of £172bn. That is the government's 35% share of the £493bn which would be produced if the economy was not distorted by Treadmill Taxes. *£172bn is more than enough to cover the shortfall in spending on schools and hospitals.* These numbers, it is important to note, are no more than a starting point for the discussion on the losses which governments wilfully impose on their constituents. In subsequent chapters we will indicate that the scale of the cumulative losses are now beyond calculation.

The May government will need time to effect change. The transition schedule is described in Chapter 3. But a Health Warning is warranted: the longer the transition, the greater the losses, the deeper the crises afflicting communities.

Many people will pay with their lives for political prevarication: their years on earth truncated by agonising over whether to remedy the legacy problems that blighted people's lives in the past.

Rent is the net (taxable) income

The seemingly intractable economic and social problems stem from conflicts that originate at the interface between private lives and the public domain. The site of conflict is the arena defined by dysfunctional taxes. The hostilities result in two negative outcomes. First, governments are constrained from fulfilling their promises. Second, people are prevented from leading the lives of their choosing. The political challenge is to convert those conflicts into the creative synergy that would flow when all parts of society are synchronised on terms that are fair for everyone. But what is meant by "fair", a word that is abused by politicians?

Democracy and good governance are achieved when two conditions are met.

1. Policy-makers honour their obligation to be transparent and accountable in the way they raise and spend the public's revenue.

2. Citizens fulfil their obligation to pay for the services they want to share in common, as delivered through their public agencies.

Over the past 300 years the people who occupied Parliament worked systematically to subvert both these conditions. There was clear intent behind that agenda: to privilege the landed aristocracy who occupied the seats of power.

Box 1:2 **The fatal 100 years**

The process of impoverishing the population of England on a class basis began under Henry VIII and his grab of monastic lands in the 1530s, which quickly led to the creation of the commercial land market. Over the following century, the aristocracy grabbed power over the public purse. The outcome was the sharp breakdown of the population into classes. To arrive at the correct remedial policies, however, it is important to examine the evidence in terms of the distribution of factor incomes rather than class formation, as is illustrated by the rise in wealth of the yeoman class.

Over the course of those 100 years, the real value of wages of working peasants was reduced. The incomes of the yeomen – composed of both wages and rents – rose rapidly. According to Alexandra Shepard's unique analysis of the evidence, by taking inflation into account, the purchasing power of the income of yeomen rose tenfold, while the value of the wages of labourers declined.* This was the beginning of the shift of England's national income from the hands of the many to the hands of the few; a process that can only be explained by the political decisions taken by those with their hands on the public purse.

* Alexandra Shepard (2016), *Accounting for Oneself: Worth, Status and the Social Order in Early Modern England*, Oxford: Oxford University Press.

Revenue raised by the traditional Land Tax was incrementally reduced in favour of taxes that fell on the incomes of peasants and then, in the 19th century, on the incomes of urban factory workers (see Box 1:2).

Doctrines were devised to rationalise the fiscal fraud inflicted on the nation. A High Finance was invented that had more to do with the three-card trick than the classical theories developed by moral philosophers like Adam Smith. The outcome, today, is the loss of collective understanding of the nature of taxable income. That knowledge needs to be recovered if people are to appreciate how they were duped into believing that the modern tax system is 'progressive'.

If governments wish to avoid creating trouble for the nation, the general rule is that they need to restrict the collection of revenue from one source: the net income produced in the economy. Taxable income is technically called economic rent. We all contribute to the production of this value through our engagement in the social side of our lives. Rent is the stream of income which remains after deducting the wages of labour and the profits of capital. Taxing any other stream of income (wages or profits) is futile. Why? A tax which initially falls on wages is shifted so that, ultimately, it is at the expense of the rent that people would otherwise pay for the use of public services. That much was affirmed long ago by philosophers including John Locke and Adam Smith. Without being conscious of it, we observe the economic logic of this process at work every day, most visibly in the housing market. When taxes on incomes or consumption are raised, we read in the media that the rate of increase of house prices has weakened. When those taxes are reduced – *lo and behold!* the property industry is aglow with the news that house prices are rising. In other words, taxes on wages and profits are an *indirect* way of collecting revenue from rents. This process goes by the acronym ATCOR – *All Taxes Come Out of Rent* – which will be fully elaborated in later chapters.

On symptoms and causes

The indirect way of collecting the economy's taxable income, or rent, dislocates communities in a thousand and one ways. Most visibly –

▶ *land* is held vacant or under-used, as speculators calculate the greater capital gains they can accumulate in the future;

▶ *labour* is rendered unemployable when employers cannot cover the cost of tax on top of wages paid to employees; and

▶ *capital* formation is distorted in favour of "tax-efficient" investments, which reduces productivity and the welfare of consumers.

Each of these three categories may be further deconstructed to expose the many terrible distortions that are imposed on people's well-being. In calculating those distortions, American professor of economics Nicolaus Tideman demonstrated that the optimum fiscal policy is not neutral. It is better than neutral, in that it rewards the efficient use of land, labour and capital.[1] By restructuring the tax regime, government – working in partnership with the people – would get to the heart of the socially significant problems that blight society. But that is not how those in power perceive their role. Social scientists have persuaded policy-makers to believe that each problem requires a dedicated solution. This is the piecemeal approach to addressing the stress points in the economy and in people's private lives. It is also the one that has not worked. And so, before the May Government can proceed to rethink political strategy, a major exercise is needed in re-examining the assumptions of economic and political philosophy. That should begin by differentiating symptoms from causes.

If the over-arching problem is one of income distribution – obscene wealth received by the 1%, abject poverty at the bottom – what would it take to rebalance the way income is produced and shared? Let us examine this issue in terms of the classical breakdown of the three factors that produce and receive the nation's income. Table 1 displays the three factors in separate columns, along with the classic formulation of the income received by each category: wages, profits and rents. But adding up the incomes received by those three agencies of production does not reveal the total income, because taxes are deducted and transferred to government, to be spent on "public goods". So the "take-home" pay of employees is net of the income tax and the payroll tax (National Insurance Contributions). Capital is subject to taxes, as is the rent received by Land.

One version of the UK's income is provided by the sum of the first four columns in Table 1:1. In the 12 months up to the first quarter of 2016 it was £1.8 trillion. HM Treasury would like to leave that number as the end of the story. But what about the Fifth Column? This identifies the income that the UK *could* have produced, given current endowments of land, labour and capital, if government had raised its revenue via direct charges on rents. Economists have a term for this foregone income: opportunity cost. Deadweight losses are that part of the UK's income that government chooses to forgo in favour of raising revenue via Income Tax, Corporation Tax, VAT and all the other Treadmill Taxes in the armoury of the Treasury. These taxes deprived the UK of *circa* £493bn, using an average "excess burden" ratio of 1:1. That is, distortions cause a loss to the economy of £1 for every £1 raised by those revenue tools that I call Treadmill Taxes. Some economists have estimated that the losses are more like £2 for every £1 collected in taxes.[2]

For whatever reason, governance is driven by a preference to employ tax methods that deprive Britain of wealth and welfare equivalent to about £493bn every year.

1 T. Nicolaus Tideman (1999), "Taxing Land is Better than Neutral: Land Taxes, Land Speculation and the Timing of Development," in Ken Wenzer (ed.), Land-Value Taxation: *The Equitable and Efficient Source of Public Finance*, Armonk, NY: M.E. Sharpe. http://schalkenbach.org/rsf-2/wp-content/uploads/2014/07/Tideman-1995-Taxing-land-better-than-neutral.pdf
2 Fred Harrison (2016), "The $14 trillion Lift-off from the Great Stagnation", in *Rent Unmasked*, London: Shepheard-Walwyn, pp. 126-129.

Table 1:1 **Full-cost accounting: UK national income**				
Labour	**Capital**	**Land**	**Government**	**Deadweight Losses**
Wages	Profits	Rents	Tax Revenue	Assuming average ratio of 1:1 **£493 bn**
minus Income Tax *minus* NICs *minus* Council Tax *minus...*	*minus* Corporation Tax *minus* Business Rates *minus...*	*minus* Taxes	(HMRC and Municipal): £588 bn (2015/16)	
National income: £1.8 trillion			**Total potential income: £2.3 trillion**	

Libertarians would reject this fiscal approach to judging the efficiency of the economy. In doing so, they create a controversy that can only be resolved by distinguishing between symptoms and causes.

Champions of the present tax regime claim that the fundamental barriers to prosperity are to be found in other institutions and practises. On taxation, they do call for a lower tax-take ("smaller government" is equated with virtue). But they oppose the abolition of Treadmill Taxes in favour of the one source of revenue which would maximise personal freedom and deliver honest governance.[3] We need to look closer at what they claim are the barriers to prosperity.

▶ In the land market, *the planning system* is identified as the prime obstacle to the supply of new houses on a scale that would satisfy demand and stabilise prices at levels people can afford.

▶ In the labour market, *trade unions* are accused of creating the frictions that curtail the ability of employers to negotiate wages at market-clearing levels which would eliminate unemployment.

▶ In the capital market, *regulatory systems* are treated as constraints on entrepreneurs; constraining (for example) the financial sector from efficiently supplying funds to facilitate production.

Vocal critics (and these include many non-governmental organisations) keep governments busy with unremitting attacks on these institutional arrangements

---

3 There are exceptions. One was the late Milton Friedman, a leading exponent of the Chicago School of economics who called the land tax "the least bad tax": quoted in Fred Harrison (1983), *The Power in the Land*, London: Shepheard-Walwyn, p.299. Friedman lived to confess his regret for the role he played in advocating the Income Tax instead of a reformed property tax.

within the markets. Palliatives are piled on new layers of palliatives in the attempt to build affordable homes and eliminate unemployment. And yet, these problems appear to have a life of their own: *they won't go away!*

There is an obvious problem with the claim that these institutions and practices are the cause of problems in the economy and society. Chronologically, they came into existence as an attempt to rectify previously existing problems. The economy, and society at large, was already in an unbalanced state. Something else was already at work to discourage optimum levels of operational efficiency. The underlying problem remains undetected because the analysts choose to fixate on symptoms. And yet, they know that trades unions emerged long after the problem of mass unemployment and low wages had disfigured British society. They know that the planning system was instituted in 1947 precisely because pre-war housing developments were driven by land speculation to sprawl into the countryside.

> For whatever reason, governance is driven by a preference to employ tax methods that deprive Britain of wealth and welfare equivalent to about £493bn every year.

Cause and effect was ignored when the last major experiment in social engineering was initiated by Margaret Thatcher. In 1986, she de-regulated the financial sector. Was efficiency in the allocation of funds improved? Concurrent with the Big Bank in the City of London, we observe the dismantling of the influence of trades unions. Did this improve the condition of labour? Did the capital and labour markets reward people with higher profits and wages? They did not. Deregulation *did* provoke the biggest of all property booms, and the banking crisis of 2008 was the outcome. The financial sector proved incapable of sustaining the services it provided to customers, and had to turn to government for salvation.

▶ Under light-touch regulation, the quantum of capital needed by a dynamic economy had shrunk.

▶ Real wages declined for the majority of people, and productivity dropped below the levels achieve in France, Germany and the USA.[4]

---

4 According to HM Treasury: "A large and long-standing productivity gap exists between the UK and other major advanced economies. Output per hour in the UK was 17 percentage points below the G7average, 27 percentage points below France, 28 percentage points below Germany and 31 percentage points below the US in 2013". https://www.gov.uk/government/publications/summer-budget-2015/summer-budget-2015

So, we need an answer to the question posed by Nobel laureate Joseph Stiglitz: "What is going on?" If we cannot blame trade unions and regulation, how do we account for the dysfunctional nature of the UK economy?

Stiglitz provided a neat summary of the problem in a lecture at Birkbeck College, London, on 3 March, 2016. For the convenience of Treasury economists, the lecture was filmed and is available on YouTube. The point of the lecture was simple: the starting point for policy reform is a clear understanding of the difference between wealth and capital.

> ' The question is, 'What is going on?' Wealth is going up, capital is actually going down relative to income. What is the difference between wealth and capital? The difference...is the capitalised value of rents. You know all about this very well here in London. The value of land is going up. Do you have more land because you have more valuable land? No. If the price of land in Southampton or in the Riviera goes up, the wealth goes up as we measure it, but capital stock could be going down, and if you actually look at the data that is actually what's been happening, relative to income. So what is going on? The wedge between the two is the capitalised value of rents. Land rents are the most obvious example, you can see that, but there are also monopoly rents. There are rents that people get by exploitation of other consumers or exploitation of the government. So the banks, when they get a bail-out, the present discounted value of the bail-out rents is capitalised in the stock market. So wealth goes up, it looks like society is wealthier. It's not. Citizens' wealth has gone down. The present discounted value of their future taxes has gone up, but we don't record that. We only record the value of the stock market. If you have more monopoly power, stock market wealth goes up, but the real income of workers goes down.'[5]

The analysis by Stiglitz is supported by the knowledge he accumulated while serving as chief economist at the World Bank and as chairman of the US President's Council of Economic Advisers. He is currently Professor of Economics at Columbia University. So when he uses the emotive word "exploitation", he does so with insight.

We need to ask: Why do democratic governments allow people to accumulate wealth by exploiting others, or by exploiting government itself?

The concept is deployed to characterise the kinds of rents that flow from the exercise of privileged or monopoly power. So we need to ask: Why do democratic governments allow people to accumulate wealth by exploiting others, or by exploiting government itself? Governments have had ample opportunity since

---

5 Joseph Stiglitz (2016), "Rewriting the Rules of the Market Economy to Achieve Shared Prosperity", London, March 3. https://www.youtube.com/watch?v=ZyKkmzgge90

1986 to answer this question. Could it be that they refused to do so, because responsibility lies exclusively with them? They write the rules – the laws of the land – to which citizens and corporations conform. If there is scope for "arbitrage" – exploiting the rules for profit – blame must rest with those who write (or refuse to rewrite) the rules. We shall set aside the issue of responsibility, at this point, to ask the question for which we need a firm answer if Brexit is to become the launch pad for a brighter future for Britain. Why would shifting taxes off wages and profits and onto rents result in a balanced economy and healthy society?

The Annual Ground Rent

The post-Brexit blueprint rests on the traditional approach to raising revenue to defray the costs of administering the State. There is little that is new in the proposal to base revenue on rent. The logic was elegantly described by Adam Smith in 1776:

> ' Both ground-rents and the ordinary rent of land are a species of revenue which the owner, in many cases, enjoys *without any care or attention of his own*. Though a part of this revenue should be taken from him in order to defray the expenses of the state, *no discouragement will thereby be given to any sort of industry*. The annual produce of the land and labour of the society, the real wealth and revenue of the great body of the people, might be the same after such a tax as before. Ground-rents, and the ordinary rent of land, are, therefore, perhaps, the species of revenue which can best bear to have a peculiar tax imposed upon them.' [6]

Refashioned for the modern era – as Stiglitz notes, there are many more ways, now, to generate rents – this model of public finance would deliver results that were organic in their social and economic effects. The honest way of raising revenue favours the well-being of everyone willing to work for a living. No-one would be excluded by the legal or financial barriers which divide the UK into Haves and Have-nots. That is the harsh lesson that remains to be learnt by the European Union. Dishonest taxation is the ultimate source of the failure of the European project.

Dishonest taxation is the ultimate source of the failure of the European project.

Is the UK capable of meeting the political challenge? Optimism is warranted, for Britain has once again been thrust onto the cusp of history. According to research by the Organisation for Economic Cooperation and Development, the world economy is pivoting on a precipice. The OECD says that "structural

---

6 *The Wealth of Nations* (1776), Canaan edn., 1976, Chicago: University of Chicago Press, Bk.V: 370; emphasis added.

reforms" are required to reverse the trend into which the world is now locked, a 50-year slowdown of the global economy.[7] The prognosis is bad. If economic activity really is gradually grinding down to a pace below what is needed to meet the needs of an expanding and aging population, history tells us that the geopolitical stresses will be relieved by outbreaks of State-driven violence. The OECD's proposals to reverse the trend are futile. It proposes strategies that are culled from within the current economic paradigm. If implemented, they would further fragment social bonds, reduce real living standards, increase the profits of rent-seeking asset owners and inflict further damage on the fabric of society. The UK could lead the way out of this global catastrophe.

Brexit has rendered redundant the default posture in politics: *"do nothing"*. Existing policies, pursued by governments around the world, have failed. Their strategy has been to shift responsibility for the 2008 crisis onto central bankers. But the stream of monetary initiatives have not delivered renewed and sustainable growth, according to William White, who chairs the OECD's economic and development review committee. He has now concluded:

' We need a paradigm shift in thinking about how the economy and policy works'.[8]

The UK is now obliged to develop new strategies of the kind that would ring-fence itself against the global dangers. New knowledge is not required: there are no mysteries to be solved. The challenges that confront our world can only be met by political determination to apply effective policies, the core one being what Adam Smith termed the Annual Ground Rent.

7 Henrik Braconier *et al.* (2014), *Policy Challenges in the Next 50 Years*, Paris: OECD.
8 William White (2016), "Only government action can resolve a global solvency crisis", *Financial Times*, September 26.

Legacy of the aristocracy

Europe is locked in the perverse value system of the land lords who shaped European civilisation out of the ashes of the Roman Empire. The founding fathers of the new Europe failed to exorcise that legacy. It is against this history that the UK and the EU need to scope out a holistic programme of action which encompasses morality, psychology and sociology, as well as economics. These all converge on an awesome challenge: how to exorcise the fiscal regime that pits government against the people in a continuous civil war.

The tax regime is encrusted with myths such as "progressivity" of income tax and the "fairness" of a "broadly-based" system. These notions emerged to rationalise the tensions in a fiscal system which privileged rents; which, in the past, drove nations to war. Mason Gaffney portrays this conflict in these terms: "The effect is like a 'scorched-earth' policy, but not one we inflict on the invading enemy in wartime: we inflict it on ourselves in all times, war and peace, by adopting a suppressive tax policy".[1]

Understanding the aristocracy's rent-seeking culture is one approach to redefining the fiscal system fit for the 21st century. Evidence for the pressure points in need of therapeutic treatment is laid bare by 5,000 years of history. The intimate relationship between land grabbing, rent appropriation, tax dodging and the propensity of the nobility to resort to war is documented by John Kautsky in *The Politics of Aristocratic Empires*.

He summarises the culture of the nobility thus:

For aristocrats to pay taxes would defeat the very purpose of government in aristocratic empires. It is, after all, to enable the aristocracy, which is the government, to take from and not give to the rest of the population, notably the peasantry.[2]

The drive to accumulate rents was inextricably linked to land grabbing. Kautsky notes that "aristocratic ideological justifications of war continue to have a powerful influence on the behaviour of governments in Europe and perhaps particularly in Germany well into the 20th century". The calls to honour and glory were central to "the thinking of the Germany aristocracy and hence also of the Nazis, whose relationship to the aristocracy was one of both admiration and resentment".

Relating this analysis to circumstances in the second half of the 20th century, we would have been driven to predict

---

1 Mason Gaffney (2009), "The Hidden Taxable Capacity of Land", *International J. of Social Economics*, 36(4), p.379.

2 John H. Kautsky (1982), *The Politics of Aristocratic Empires*, Chapel Hill: University of North Carolina Press, p.155.

the resurgence of fascism. The aristocracy as a politically influential class has disappeared, but its rent-seeking behaviour continues to pervade society. Is it a coincidence that the dominance of the rent-seeking culture is associated with the resurgence of far-right political parties, and a far-left reaction? People who feel besieged are vulnerable and some are attracted to fascist sentiments. The reawakening of these sentiments has coalesced around a new scapegoat: the Muslim community.

- A former German finance ministry and central bank official identifies Muslims as Enemy No 1, with refugees from Near East wars said to be diluting German culture. "Winning back control over our borders," he writes, "will be an existential question for our culture and the survival of our society."[3]

- The outbreak of violence is the usual culmination of a long period of social exploitation, discontent and the build-up of animosities expressed as communal strife. According to senior politicians in Europe, the continent is now witnessing the return of Weimar Republic-like conditions.

- Brexit offers the opportunity to forestall the historic consequences of war. The Brits, in the course of their Article 50 negotiations, can hold out a vision of the future that works for the EU as well as the UK.

The current social models in countries like Greece and Spain are not working. Failure is measured by relatively low levels of consumption, saving and investment. The task for UK negotiators is to provide a coherent account of how governments caused the profligate waste of capital (most visibly so in the form of resources locked up in ghost towns - Spain, like Ireland, endured this form of resource waste during the years of land speculation prior to 2008).

Symptoms of the failed model of governance include the State-sponsored abuse of natural habitats (caused by public pricing policies which reward behaviour that damages the environment). In explaining the need for a mutually beneficial agreement, the UK could demonstrate how the EU's open seas policy caused the decimation of fishing communities in England and Scotland. The common fisheries policy (CFP) was supposed to nurture competition on equal terms. But the small family-owned fishing vessels were no match for the corporate-owned trawlers that dredged the bottom of the seas. Greenpeace notes:

[O]ver 70% of fish stocks are overfished. The CFP favours the most powerful parts of the fishing industry, with the highest environmental impact. Many boats using unsustainable, often destructive, methods have been awarded fishing rights (quota) and have received billions in taxpayer subsidies. This has resulted in companies building bigger boats, capable of catching even more fish. This fleet is so powerful that it can catch two to three times more fish than the ocean can handle.[4]

Anchored in the annual ground rent policy is the doctrine of responsible behaviour that does not tolerate such vandalism.

---

3 Thilo Sarrazin (2016), *Wunschdenken*, Stuttgart: Deutsche Verlags-Anstalt. Reviewed by Stefan Wagstyl (2016), "A homage to Germany before the immigrants", *Financial Times*, July 4.

4 http://www.greenpeace.org.uk/oceans/fishing-laws-need-fixing

2

The Gravity Model

THE GOVERNMENTS of Europe failed after the First World War, with the Treaty of Versailles, and they failed again, after the Second World War, when they signed the Treaty of Rome in 1957. Those treaties did not enshrine the principles that would lead to the rebalancing of relationships between nations on terms that were capable of delivering peace and prosperity for everyone. In fact, the statesmen who negotiated the two post-war settlements did so from within the architecture of power that nourished the seeds of conflict. No attempt was made to isolate the causes of territorial wars. Instead, they resorted to a crude strategy: aggregate power on a sufficient scale to deter the prospect of another war. That allowed whatever it was that disrupts harmony between populations to recover and mutate, free to strike when the conditions were ripe.

Brexit has provided both the UK, and Europe, with the opportunity to go back to the beginning. But early indications did not suggest a willingness to question the assumptions which anchor the traditional views of how the world works.

In the UK, those who wished to remain within the EU continued to treat membership as the best-of-all-worlds option. They gravitated towards a negotiating position for Brexit on the old terms - access to the "free market". No attempt was made to animate the collective imagination with visions of new horizons. Instead, it was more of the same pessimism; the kind that led Alastair Darling, who was Chancellor of the Exchequer when the 2008 crisis struck, to report that he was more worried by Brexit than the episode that bust Britain's banks.

' The world's banking system was within hours of collapse. But I could see what to do. [Prime Minister] Gordon Brown and I were able to put in place a £500 billion rescue plan overnight. It worked.' [1]

If £500 billion could be mustered overnight to save the banks, couldn't such an operation be launched to rescue the UK? But Britain did not need rescuing: it was not about to collapse. The dark prognoses, which included the prospect of war, were nourished by a poverty of philosophy and imagination.

---

1 Alistair Darling (2016), "I am more worried now than I was in 2008 crisis", *The Mail on Sunday*, June 26.

The Big Four – HM Treasury, the Institute for Fiscal Studies, the IMF and the OECD – were equally pessimistic. They deployed the same economic assumptions to arrive at identical conclusions: catastrophe would follow if the UK lost access to the EU's marketplace. To varying degrees they emphasised that wages would decline, jobs would be lost, taxes would have to be raised (or public spending cut) and Britain would lose its political influence in the world. But something was missing from their calculations. That is why they concluded that each household would lose £4,300 a year if Britain strayed outside the EU. And so, as the context for assessing how to rebalance the UK economy and society, we need to briefly revisit the assumptions of those who were willing to trade British sovereignty for the succour of EU membership.

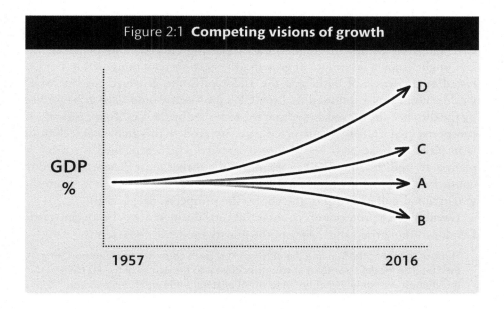

Figure 2:1 **Competing visions of growth**

To help us visualise alternative outcomes, four scenarios are stylised in Figure 2:1. Scenario A represents what actually happened to the UK. This, the Remainers contended, was the optimum position. According to their logic, had Britain not joined the European Community in 1973, her economic condition would have deteriorated below the level that was actually achieved (Scenario B). The Remainers made no attempt to assess the costs against the benefits of membership, to determine the net effect. They did not compute, for example, the economic and social losses that must be attributed to EU fishing policy, which decimated ancient coastal communities from the top of Scotland down to the south-east of England. No attempt was made to calculate the losses to the inland communities in which European migrants concentrated. Their presence heightened the stress on housing stocks and welfare facilities, pressures that would intensify as the five low-income candidate countries secured membership of the EU: Albania (average net monthly wage: €357), Macedonia (€358), Montenegro (€488), Serbia (€366) and Turkey (€584). The UK would undoubtedly lure people from those countries. No attempt was made by the Remainers to estimate the costs in terms of the demands on education and health services, provisions for which were being curbed by the need to balance government budgets.

There may have been a net gain from all of these interactions, but the Remainers declined to add up the costs to offset against the benefits. If they had done so, they would have had to take account of the losses attributable to EU red tape, which reduced the UK's productivity. According to the UK government's regulatory impact assessments, the cost of the top 100 EU-derived regulations was around £33.3 billion per year.[2]

Nor was consideration given to Scenario C: the possibility that, outside the EU, and even within the framework of existing customs and practices, the UK might enjoy a faster rate of growth. The case for remaining within the EU rested on an article of faith: that the Treaty of Rome delivered the best of all worlds. From this it followed that the UK's prospects would have to be gauged by the distance she moved away from the terms set by the EU. To measure those prospects, HM Treasury constructed a gravity model. This analytical technique is inspired by Isaac Newton's theory of gravity, which explained the orbit of planets around the sun. The key assumption was that most benefits accrued to countries that cruised within the EU orbit. And so, the further away from the gravitational pull of Brussels, the poorer the prospects (Scenario B).

David Blake, a professor of economics at Cass Business School City University London, summarised the theory of the gravity model in these terms:

' Think of the EU as the Sun and the different European countries as planets orbiting the Sun. The model assumes that countries closest to the centre of the EU have the greatest economic benefits – in terms of bilateral trade and foreign direct investment and their subsequent effects on productivity and economic growth – from membership of the EU.'

Logically, this meant that countries within Euroland would enjoy the greatest benefits. That is not how events turned out. Countries that joined the Euro heartland suffered the most, compared to EU members who remained outside euroland. *The stronger the gravitational pull towards Brussels, the greater the risks, as the populations on the southern rim of Europe discovered to their great cost.*

But what would be the UK's fate if membership of the EU was cancelled? The terms of the gravity model were scrutinised by Prof Blake. He found that they were dishonestly rigged to generate politically convenient conclusions.

' The specific gravity model used by the Treasury is centred on the EU: this model predicts that the UK would actually be better off not only staying in the EU but

2 http://openeurope.org.uk/today/blog/whats-best-way-cutting-33-3bn-burden-eu-red-tape/

actually joining the euro – although the Treasury does not acknowledge this. Had the Treasury used a different gravity model centred on the rest of the world – which it certainly should have considered – it might well have found that the UK would be better off leaving the EU.'[3]

The Treasury's gravity model was an exercise in state-sponsored propaganda. Unable to contain his anger at the manipulation of theory and statistics to mislead people, Prof Blake concluded:

'There was a time when the global plutocracy relied on the mysticism of religion to keep the populace in its place. Now the modern global plutocracy is using the mysticism of economic models. The wrath of God has been replaced by the wrath of a gravity model. If we fall for this, we will enter a new Dark Age where fear over the size of the EU trade dummy in a gravity model is intended to keep us all under control.'

The majority of people did not fall for the trick. Warned that their economic prospects diminished, the further they strayed from EU influence, they decided to put the pessimistic predictions to the test. And as it happens, the world did not come to an end the day after Brexit was formally announced as the democratic will of the people of Britain.

But what lay in wait beyond Brexit? Is there a viable Scenario D, a route to an even better future? Back in the 1960s, instead of trying to lock into the European orbit, might the UK have launched herself into an entirely new universe of prosperity?

Creating a new universe

A different kind of world awaits the UK. The take-off into a new universe would result if the nation embarked on an orbit away from the gravitational pull of the policies created in days of yore by those who replaced the traditional Land Tax with Treadmill Taxes. From a standing start, within the lifetime of one Parliament the UK economy could be growing above the historical trend by at least an extra 2% per annum. This prediction is based on an enormous cache of empirical evidence which was ignored by the gravity modellers at HM Treasury.

In the past, countries that executed this feat – switching to the direct collection of revenue from their economy's net income – reaped the rewards in the form of enormous leaps in growth. I confined my assessment of the UK's future by taking into account the performance of five cases.

▶ *Denmark:* In 1916, the value of land was assessed separately from capital improvements, and fiscal policies were introduced whose gravitational pull was away from land speculation and towards value-adding enterprise.

---

3 David Blake (2016), *Measurement without Theory: On the extraordinary abuse of economic models in the EU Referendum debate*, London: Cass Business School City University, 9 June, p.2.

A landmark political event occurred in 1957 with the election of the Ground Duty Government. Ole Lefmann and Karsten Larsen analysed the impact on the affairs of what was then still a country relatively poor in natural resources (North Sea oil rents were to come on-stream much later). The government deficit was replaced by a surplus. Unemployment disappeared almost completely. And people enjoyed the highest real wages the country had ever known, thanks to a dramatic increase in industrial production and personal savings on the back of tax-free investments.[4] Denmark has never looked back.

▶ *Singapore:* After the island was de-colonised by Britain, Singapore passed the Land Acquisition Act (1966). Rents that accrued from the 1970s onwards were ploughed into infrastructure, and taxes that damaged the economy were held down. The annual growth rate between 1970 and 2012 was 7.6%.

Roger Sandilands, emeritus professor of economics at Glasgow's University of Strathclyde, examined the island's economy while on secondment to Singapore's National University. He calculates that, if Singapore's fiscal regime had been emulated, the UK growth rate (an annual average of 2.5%) would have been higher by at least 2%. Three times richer than Singapore in 1970, the UK ended up 17% poorer by 2011.[5] Victor Savage, an associate professor at the National University, reports that in the five decades between 1965 and 2013, Singapore increased real GDP per capita by 1,356%. The rest of the world managed to grow by 146%, and the USA lagged with a rate of 96%.[6]

▶ *Hong Kong:* The rock plugged into mainland China was leased by Britain in the 1840s. Merchants who arrived to do business could only acquire property on leasehold terms. That remained the case all the way through to 1997. A substantial part of public revenue is still collected directly from the rent of land.[7]

Hong Kong is rated the No.1 open market economy in the world, thanks to the legacy of low taxes. By drawing most of its revenue from the sale of leases, and charges on rents, the colony flourished to the point where, today, per capita income is greater than the UK's (see Table 2:1). This outcome was due to the gravitational pull towards a low-tax regime, made possible by the funding of public services out of rent.

---

4 Unless otherwise stated, this and the other case studies discussed here are drawn from R.V. Andelson (2000), *Land-Value Taxation Around the World*, 3rd edn., Oxford: Blackwell.
5 Roger Sandilands (2016), "The Culture of Prosperity", in *Rent Unmasked*, Ch.13.
6 Victor R. Savage (2015), "Singapore's Geography Does Matter: National Embeddings, Global Aspirations", p.253, in *Beyond 50: Re-imagining Singapore*, Editor: Joachim Sim, Singapore: Really Good Books. https://issuu.com/nuslkyschool/docs/beyond_50_re-imagining_singapore/254
7 Andrew Purves (2016), *No Debt High Growth Low Tax*, London: Shepheard-Walwyn.

▶ *Taiwan:* In the 1950s, Chairman Mao's Red Army drove the nationalists (the Kuomintang: KMT) from the mainland to Formosa. The first reform was the land-to-the-tiller programme. Landlords were pensioned off, and a tax on land values was introduced.

The equalisation of land rights was enshrined in the constitution to honour the doctrine formulated by the first President of the Republic of China. Sun Yat-sen became President in 1911 after the fall of the Qing dynasty. He called his doctrine the Three Principles of the People. This included the Land Tax which he had learnt about from English philosopher John Stuart Mill and American social reformer Henry George. He introduced a land-value-based tax in 1924 along with a capital gains tax to forestall land speculation. But the KMT's authority was challenged by regional warlords and Mao's Communist Party. Social stability and economic reform were undermined by the Red Army, which fought a running battle all the way through to World War 2. Finally, the KMT was forced to retreat to Formosa (which became Taiwan). The gravitational pull of the KMT's land-and-tax policies turned the island into the 1st Asian Tiger. Taiwan's per capita income in 2015 was higher than the UK's.

Table 2:1 **GDP per capita** (purchasing power parity): US$ 2015 estimates*	
United Kingdom	41,200
Denmark	45,700
Hong Kong	56,700
Taiwan	46,800
Australia	65,400
Singapore	85,300
Argentina	22,600
South Africa	13,200
* CIA Factbook: https://www.cia.gov/library/ publications/the-world-factbook/geos/as.html	

▶ *Australia:* As British migrants settled the continent in the late 19th century, they knew there was one way only to fund the infrastructure they needed: out of rent. Within a few years, all six states employed this method of raising revenue.

Australia climbed to the top of the league of exporting countries at the beginning of the 20th century. A graduated federal land tax was introduced in 1910, designed to break up large estates. Over the past 100 years, attempts were made to renege on the fiscal doctrine that laid the foundations of the continent's prosperity. Even so, while the federal land tax was abolished in 1952, all states continue to employ a land tax.

In none of these cases was the pure AGR model applied on a consistent basis to remove all taxes that impose artificial ceilings on productivity. Consequently, for example, in the case of Australia, house prices remain a problem. Nonetheless, the performance of these countries has been exemplary compared with the UK. By estimating the gravitational effects of the AGR model, we are left in no doubt about the positive gains to be achieved as a result of implementing the Brexit blueprint. But can we cross-check this conclusion?

Reversing away from AGR

Two countries *backed away* from raising revenue directly from rents. They endured economic set-backs for two primary reasons:

1. They adopted taxes that burdened labour and capital; and

2. they misallocated their rich endowment of natural assets, resulting in mass unemployment of labour, huge swathes of fertile land left idle, and property speculation. This was the recipe for a severe drop in productivity.

▶ *Argentina:* In the 1820s the leasehold system of allocating land was adopted. This made it possible to raise revenue from rent and abolish taxes and trade tariffs. Had these policies remained in place, the newly-settled country would have flourished alongside Australia as a high-income exporting country.

Fiscal incentives favoured an expansion of employment in the agricultural sector. Argentina's diplomatic envoy, Dr Ignacio Núñez, explained the logic of this strategy to the British government: "The present taxes bear harmfully upon the people and hinder development...The rent of land is the most solid and definite source of revenue on which the State must count".[8] But the intrusion of a dictator in 1835 threw the process into reverse. The inflow of rent into the public purse stalled. Land allocation policies were steadily eroded in favour of the creation of large, under-utilised plantations. Argentina went into slow decline. The outcome was a country that defaulted on $82 billion in sovereign bonds in 2002, and a per capita income one-third of Australia's (Table 2:1).

▶ *South Africa:* Site-value rating was introduced in 1916. By the end of the century 70% of city revenue was collected from the rent of sites, while exempting the value of buildings.

With the end of apartheid, the benefits of urban prosperity could have been shared with the indigenous population. Instead, in 2004 the ANC government decided to terminate the collection of revenue directly from the rent of land alone. It adopted the UK property tax, which fell on the joint value of land and buildings. This contravened the letter and the spirit of the constitution, which states in the Preamble that "South Africa belongs to all who live in it". The outcome of the 2004 decision was a boom in urban land prices and the concentration of ever more unemployed people in shanty towns.

8 Quoted in Fred Harrison (2008), The Silver Bullet, London: TheIU, p.140.

Common sense

The foregoing evidence may be tested against the reader's personal experiences, drawing on observations of what happened in the UK during the last 18-year business cycle (1992-2010). Over that period, and with increasing intensity, the public's revenue gravitated further away from ground rents as governments ramped up their taxes on wages and profits. Fiscal bias diverted resources towards property speculation (in the name of helping people to "get on the property ladder") and away from value-adding activities. This continued until land prices peaked in 2007. The impact was visible in

▶ *corrosion* of the labour market (declining real wages)

▶ *erosion* of the skills base (*hysteresis*)

▶ *decay* of fixed capital (decreasing productivity) and

▶ *deficits* in government finances (austerity imposed on low-income families).

Combining this history into an enriched gravity model, we are able to predict that a reformed revenue system would escalate Britain into full employment and rising real value of wages, and a quality of life for everyone that would be unique in the history of the British Isles. This social universe contrasts starkly with the one within which the 27 members of the EU continue to rotate.

The culture of inspiration

Before mandating fiscal reform, people need a strong sense of the quality (rather than just the numbers) of the transformation that would ensue. Correctly implemented, the AGR model renders possible nothing less than a renaissance, a qualitative shift in culture in its broadest sense. Fiscal policy is converted from a tool of exploitation into the organising mechanism for wonderful outcomes that people would be free to select for themselves. In the process of unwinding the negative effects of the current tax regime, it would quickly become clear how lives had been impoverished materially, spiritually, morally and aesthetically. The despair that was enshrined in the policies on which the EU was built evokes visions of the psychological obstacles to the good life. Instead of solid foundations of prosperity, the founding fathers preserved the conditions that result in social division and poverty. This indicates the scale of the mountain that has to be climbed, if the UK is to forge a new settlement based on inclusive prosperity.

The starting point is the financial formula that made civilisation possible. The ancient Egyptians were the first to work out the methodology for measuring the net income produced by people who worked in the fields on the banks of the Nile. That net income could be safely collected without repressing people's willingness to work, to save, to invest and innovate. By tailoring the revenue system to exempt wages and the returns on investments, the divisions that afflict communities today would steadily evaporate. What works for relationships between individuals would also serve to rebalance the relationships between nations. The social and environmental effects would be electrifying. Some of the major outcomes are highlighted in Figure 2:2.

▶ *Citizenship would be rooted in responsibility.* Today, through no fault of their own, fiscal law sanctions people to engage in get-rich practises at the expense of others.

▶ *Governance would rest on accountability.* Today, governments spend tax revenue without being held responsible for how benefits are used.

▶ *High Finance would become transparent.* Today, the benefits from public investments are covertly distributed to land owners as "windfalls".

▶ *Economics would conform to ethics.* Today, the laws of the land reward materialistic behaviour without regard for moral sensibilities.

Transforming the character of the public's finance would enrich communities and natural habitats. But to achieve this outcome, the transition has to be carefully planned to avoid seizure of the financial system.

Figure 2:2 **The AGR model as organising mechanism**

Sponge effect of the land market

The process that concentrates resources in large metropolitan centres like London, Dublin and Paris is called agglomeration. Outcomes would not be problematic if the organic fiscal system was in place.[1] When the public's revenue is derived from the annual ground rent, a self-correcting mechanism kicks in to ensure equilibrium at all levels of society. This results when the heightened net gains (rents) are correctly shared with everyone and every location within the economy. The failure to pool the rents results in the malformation of the social system. Two features illuminate how the land market operates as a sponge to squeeze rents from the regions in favour of the owners of land in the social centres.

The magnetic effects of the metropolis are exaggerated under the influence of an unbalanced fiscal system. One perverse consequence is demographic: people are driven out of the regions and into the centre. They become involuntary migrants (in the 17th century they were vilified as "vagabonds").

- People in the outer regions, like the Western Isles of Scotland or the North-east of England, are displaced from their birthplaces as the economic vitality of their local economies is exhausted.

- Migrants head for Madrid or Rome. These urban locations then sprawl into the countryside in response to land speculation, which drives the price of houses to unaffordable levels.

- As public services become over-burdened, the call goes out for more investment in infrastructure such as transport, which obliges government to raise taxes even further.

The cumulative effects are self-defeating. Increases in the tax-take become a self-devouring process which accelerates the damage to the fabric of all communities. New fiscal burdens fall more heavily on the outer regions, adding further twists to the out-migration. The history of Ireland is a tragic illustration. For 200 years, young people were forced to flee their homeland in search of work. Then, in the 1990s, the perverse tax regime that was designed to attract foreign corporations created the illusion of prosperity. The Celtic Tiger, as the boom was dubbed, clawed its way into two human disasters:

---

1 Fred Harrison (2016), *As Evil Does*, London: Geophilos.

- **displaced** Irish citizens were attracted back from their foreign havens in the belief that they could relocate and build the future of their families back home; and

- **house prices** took off. The default response to perverse taxation: land speculation on an epic scale, as entrepreneurs are bitten by the get-rich-quick bug.

The outcome was heartbreaking. When the economy crashed in 2008, out-migration resumed; and the landscape was blighted by ghost towns — half-completed dwellings that no-one wanted. The Irish government had failed to understand that the land market is a mechanism for transferring value. Owners of land have the greatest bargaining power, because their asset is in fixed supply. A Dublin employer can hire workers from Poland, if he needs to; and by doing so, he can drive down the wages of indigenous employees. But he cannot import land from Poland and deposit it in the middle of Dublin!

Eight years after the land-driven boom/bust that caused the bankruptcy of banks in 2008, the legacy in Ireland is a hoard of 198,000 vacant residential units in a country that claims to be short of affordable homes. Pat Doyle of the Peter McVerry Trust, a Dublin-based homeless people's charity, writes that "the enduring issues that continue to give rise to our broken housing system have yet to be solved". According to Doyle:

To achieve affordability there are two critical issues [which] Governments do not like to address, land speculation and rent regulation. Rooting out and preventing land speculation, which drives up the cost and impacts on the

availability of land for housing, is a critical cost control factor.[2]

The Irish government's housing action plan, *Rebuilding Ireland*, is fatally flawed. It makes no provision for revising the fiscal system, so the economy and society remain in permanent disequilibrium.

Driving the process which rewards land speculation is political failure: the rent-seeking culture victimises democracy.

Governments in the Welfare States of Europe covertly distribute hundreds of billions of pounds worth of tax-funded value – rents – to the privileged section of society, every year. The major beneficiaries of state-sponsored largesse are not the unemployed, the sick, the handicapped. They are the middle-class home-owners. As proprietors of small plots of land, they have become the most privileged recipients of state welfare. Much of that welfare – which surfaces in the land market as capital gains – is funded by taxpayers who, as rent-paying tenants, do not qualify for these hand-outs.

Unlike the benefits distributed to those who are in need, hand-outs to home owners — and to the owners of agricultural, commercial and industrial land — escape the monitoring process.

- The gifts are not mandated by taxpayers

- Recipients are not means-tested

- Parliaments sanction the give-aways by default

- There is no oversight of how the benefits are used

In the UK, the give-away bonanza is the greatest barrier to the government's post-Brexit aspiration: an inclusive, balanced economy.

---

2 Pat Doyle (2016), "Coming months will tell us if Government has the will to deliver on housing plan", *Irish Times*, August 30.

3

Renaissance

CAPITALISM is in Theresa May's crosshairs. Scandals like the plunder of corporate assets by unscrupulous bosses, leaving employees and pensioners high and dry; and the plunder of the public purse by entrepreneurs whose profits are then concealed in tax havens, have been revealed to public gaze. But if governments wish to remove the incentives that induce such behaviour, changes would have to be introduced to the way the nation's income is distributed. The principal tool at the disposal of government is the power of the public purse. Tax policy is the primary determinant not just of how a nation's income is shared through private markets; it also shapes the attitudes of people towards the "common good".

The starting point for an objective analysis of how to recalibrate the UK economy is with events of the day after the Brexit votes were counted. Panic was evident in the violent swings in stock markets; which, however, made up the losses within a few days. Sterling lost value against the dollar, which improved the competitiveness of British goods in foreign markets. Pollsters recorded people's state of uncertainty, but as consumers they increased their spending in the shops. The state of anxiety which surfaced had less to do with real events, and more to do with awareness that the experts were not in control of the grand narrative. If history was anything to go by, their proposals for the post-referendum era would deepen the crises that pre-dated Brexit. People's intuitions were well-founded, as was illustrated by pronouncements from two people who were responsible for delivering economic stability.

▶ Mark Carney, Governor of the Bank of England, announced that interest rates were likely to be reduced from 0.5%, (they were cut, to 0.25%). *Diminishing the returns on savings would not restore confidence, or encourage investors to risk money in capital formation (to raise productivity).*

▶ George Osborne, in what turned out to be one of his final pronouncements as Chancellor, revealed his plan to cut Corporation Tax to attract foreign investment. *Savings from a cut in Corporation Tax would, for the most part, drive up house prices even further beyond the reach of many more families.*

The immediate need was for action that would encourage people to spend, and to invest in the formation of fixed capital. Monetary policy had failed to deliver sustainable growth since 2008. The best that could be said for central bank intervention (with "quantitative easing") was that the bankers had been successfully bailed out. The costs were imposed on others, most poignantly the taxpayers and vulnerable members of society whose welfare benefits were cut. In 2016 people knew that, in policy terms, governance was in a cul-de-sac. Would politicians now turn to fiscal policy to chart a new course?

Throughout the western world the political Left (Jeremy Corbyn in the UK, Bernie Sanders in the USA, Podemos in Spain, Syriza in Greece) offered critiques of capitalism, but they could not (or would not) identify the paradigm shift that would deliver both social renewal and sustainable economic activity. They advocated more public borrowing to fund social infrastructure. That, by itself, would enrich a minority of asset owners and add another vicious downward twist to the unbalanced economy.

> Granting tax holidays to enterprises shifts bargaining power to land owners, a power that is ultimately employed to dislocate operations in the market economy.

The political Right was no better equipped to meet the historic challenge. Myopia compromised their good intentions. Tory grandee William Hague, a former leader of the Conservative Party who had served as Foreign Secretary in David Cameron's first administration, highlighted the dangerous geopolitical situation. Western nations were "in a race against time to find workable solutions before rampant populism overwhelms them". He recommended generous tax cuts for small businesses, the creation of tax-free enterprise zones, while "fair taxes from the big corporations are vital, but that shouldn't stop us going for low taxes".[1] If implemented, Hague's prospectus would be like taking a wrecking ball to the economy. We do not have to guess at the probable impact of each of his proposals, because empirical evidence has been well documented.[2] The cumulative effect is to boost land prices.

The Left and the Right failed to take into account the social consequences arising from the unique characteristics of land, the asset that is in fixed supply. Its owners exercise the power to soak up the net income relinquished by

---

1 William Hague (2016), "To pacify discontent, it's vital that we plan a bright, hi-tech future", *Daily Telegraph*, July 26.
2 Margaret Thatcher's experiment in enterprise zones, for example, was a failure. They did not create the desired number of jobs. Fred Harrison (1983), *The Power in the Land*, London: Shepheard-Walwyn, p.264-266. Similar outcomes are to be observed in China's more recent foray into tax-privileged zones.

government through tax cuts. Spending on infrastructure is imperative: but the net gains – measured by land prices in the catchment areas of such investments – are allowed to sluice into the pockets of property owners. The problem is not with the fact that net income has risen: such a rise affirms that resources were not poured in "white elephant" projects. The problem is with the failure of government to collect the net income to defray the costs of the infrastructure. Granting tax holidays to enterprises (such as those located in privileged enterprise zones) does not result in sustained growth. It shifts the bargaining power further to the advantage of land owners, a power that is ultimately employed to dislocate operations in the market economy. Understanding the sponge effect of the land market is the key to de-coding most of the failures of governance (see Box 3:1).

But can it be done?

Sticking with the devil you know is a human trait, a hedge against the risks of embarking on voyages into uncharted territory. In addressing the challenges of phasing in the AGR model, it would help to note the circumstances under which the reform was adopted in the countries that were identified in Chapter 2.

Denmark is the only case of a settled country making the rational decision to reverse the culture of rent-seeking. The country did not act under duress. A democratic choice was exercised, made possible by a century's long history of enlightened governance. In the 19th century, possessory rights to land were

---

Box 3:1 **The most sensitive barometer**

The sensitive nature of the land market was illustrated by events preceding and following the Brexit vote.

In the run-up to the referendum, newspapers reported that the housing market was volatile, especially in London. Anxieties created by those who wished the UK to remain in the EU infected property prices. Capital & Counties, the firm redeveloping a large site that once housed the Earls Court exhibition centre, provided evidence that the problem was not with "bricks and mortar" but with land values. Uncertainty in the London market had caused the value of its Earls Court site to decrease from £1.4bn in December 2015 to £1.2bn in July 2016 – a drop of 14%.*

After the referendum, sterling declined in value. Foreign buyers, armed with increased purchasing power, immediately started buying high-value properties in London's choice locations. Vendors took the opportunity to raise their prices.

Policy-makers ignore the sponge effect of the land market – the capacity to soak up or squeeze out net income – when they embark on new initiatives to address old problems. That is why the old problems keep recurring.

* Robyn Wilson (2016), "Capco slashes Earls Court value by 14% over Brexit concerns", Construction News, July 26. http://www.constructionnews.co.uk/home/capco-slashes-earls-court-value-by-14/10009156.article

granted to tenant farmers, and an extensive network of adult education schools was created in rural areas. These turned out to be essential pre-conditions for the fiscal reform that occurred in the 20th century.

In the case of Hong Kong, the British government had no choice in the matter. Because it secured the island on a lease, it could not sell freeholds to merchants. The model it was obliged to adopt, therefore, was the one familiar to the aristocracy: leasing the land on payment of AGR. *The difference was that the rents went into the colonial government's coffers and were invested in public infrastructure.*

In the case of Singapore, the former British colony had elected to become one of the 14 states of the federation of Malaysia. Frequent disagreements relating to economics, finance and politics ended the relationship in 1965, when Malaysian Prime Minister Tunku Abdul Rahman expelled Singapore from the Federation. As an independent state from 9 August 1965, the island was on its own in a hostile global world. It enacted the Land Acquisition Act in the following year.

In all the other cases, the populations were either fighting for survival (Taiwan), or they were confronted by enormous challenges as they scanned vast territories that would need a great deal of infrastructure. With no exploiting class over them, they were free to devote the net income they generated to funding their social needs. In doing so, they executed a rapid development of their economies.

Post-Brexit, the UK did not find itself under siege, but can the peoples of the British Isles afford to leave the policy choices to the whims of politicians whom they consider to have ill-served them thus far? Two considerations suggest that they will not tolerate the business-as-usual option. First, with Brexit, people affirmed their right to chart a new course into the future. Second, the AGR model is not a novel idea for Britain. Repeated attempts were made in the 20th century to reconstruct public finances on ethical foundations. Those attempts were defeated by vested interests, but people did not abandon their aspirations. Furthermore, the character that is distinctively British also needs to be taken into account. When the going gets tough, the Brits are not known for avoiding a fight. Two relevant examples illuminate their tenacious character.

In 1937, the Women's National Liberal Federation gathered for their Annual Meeting in the seaside town of Margate. They refused to be discouraged by what had happened to the land tax, which was enacted in 1931 budget, but deleted from the statute book in 1934. Still, they remained tenacious, and unanimously adopted this resolution:

' This Council of the Women's Liberal Federation re-affirms the Party's declaration that legislation should be introduced to secure that the benefit of publicly created land values should not accrue to private interests which have nothing to do with their creation but should be applied for the benefit of the community as a whole; and urges that, as the building of houses and their improvement give useful employment and increase the national wealth, the present short-sighted system of penalizing such work by an increase in rates [property tax] should be abandoned and the resulting loss to revenue be recouped by the taxation of land values.' [3]

Then, in 1939, as dark clouds gathered over Europe, Herbert Morrison, a Member of Parliament, sought to assist the London County Council in its bid to strengthen the financial foundations of the capital. London wanted its municipal revenue to be collected from site values. The London Rating (Site Values) Bill was presented as a private Bill on February 8, 1939.[4] The Speaker ruled that it raised issues of such importance that it would have to be presented as a public Bill. A week later, when Morrison submitted it as a public Bill, the House of Commons divided: Ayes, 135; Noes, 229.

The knowledge which informed those pre-war initiatives has now been lost from the collective memory, but the wisdom embedded in the national character of the British remains. The first step towards execution of the Brexit blueprint, therefore, is the renewal of the national conversation that was terminated by the terrible events which followed Germany's invasion of Poland in 1939. And with dark clouds once again gathering across the Channel, the UK cannot afford the luxury of not converting public conversation into parliamentary action.

The 5-year countdown

In framing the timetable for the Brexit blueprint, account needs to be taken of events which, under current fiscal realities, are beyond control. We start with two significant dates as they affect the politics and economics of the UK.

▶ **2019:** the halfway mark for the 18-year business cycle (2010-2028). If the cycle unfolds according to the dynamics of previous cycles, Britain crashes into recession one year before the general election of 2020.[5] The May government could defensively anticipate this prospect by explaining that - under the current fiscal regime - it does not have the capacity to head off the recession. In explaining how the land market shapes the business cycle, a mandate for change could be mobilised.

▶ **2026:** the termination point for rising land prices, which foreshadows the end of the cycle. The peak in property prices reprises what happened in 1972, 1990 and 2008. If, in the run-up to 2026, tax reform has not been completed, the depression which begins in 2028 will forestall plans for change. Governments will be too preoccupied with emergency action to mitigate the catastrophe, the damage from which will exceed what happened post-2008.

---

3 The resolution, submitted by the Cardiff and District W.L.A., was moved by Alison Garland, seconded by Lady Horsley and supported by Miss M.E. Marshall, Cardiff W.L.F., and by Mr. Atholl Robertson, ex-MP for Finchley. "Women Liberals," Land & Liberty, November 1937, p.163. Emphasis in original.

4 http://hansard.millbanksystems.com/bills/london-rating-site-values-bill

5 Fred Harrison (2005), *Boom Bust: House Prices, Banking and the Depression of 2010*, London: Shepheard-Walwyn.

These considerations suggest that the UK has, at most, a decade in which to get its affairs in order. But even as Theresa May's Brexit negotiators reviewed their plans in London, the timetable for reform in the UK was being telescoped by events unfolding in Europe. Leaders of the remaining 27 nations of the EU flew to Bratislava for an emergency meeting on September 7, 2016. They decided that, to address the "existential threats" to the union, they had to have a reform plan of their own drafted by Brussels and presented in just six months.[6] The plan would be delivered when they met in Rome in March 2017 to celebrate the 60th anniversary of the Treaty of Rome.

Just how serious were the events in Europe was stressed by Frauke Petry, leader of the Eurosceptic Alternative for Germany party. She warned that, to avoid disintegration of the EU, her country had five years to resolve the immigration and sovereignty issues. Mainstream politicians concurred. This puts the turning point in Europe's fortunes as 2021. Social tensions building within France and Germany prescribed the need for a mutually beneficial Brexit settlement, one that was dictated by the impacts of migration and the onslaught from Islamic malcontents. Taking all these considerations into account, implementation of fiscal reform in the UK needs to be compressed into a 5-year period. Can it be done?

NZ, Australia and Denmark, which routinely re-assess the value of land separately from buildings for tax purposes, would supply teams of appraisers to assist British surveyors in establishing a UK-wide database of land values and rents.

People need time to explore the implications of the AGR model. Time is also needed for the experts to de-brief themselves. And government must independently assess the impact of AGR reform on the UK, using a correctly specified gravity model. These needs could be met in the two years 2017-18. Then, armed with a democratic consensus, Parliament could authorise the practical steps to facilitate fiscal reform in 2019, launching the 2-year exercise in revaluing land. New Zealand, Australia and Denmark, which routinely re-assess the value of land separately from buildings for tax purposes, would supply teams of appraisers to assist British surveyors in establishing a UK-wide database of land values and rents. That database is needed, whether the fiscal reform takes place or not.

---

6 Stefan Wagstyl (2016), "German right-wing leader warns of EU demise", *Financial Times*, July 28.

But the pace of change would not be under the sole control of government. Reaction in the markets would be immediate to the news that government was serious about rebalancing the public's finances. Assuming that the political intentions were perceived as credible, the financial implications would be instantly registered in the land market. In the housing sector, construction companies would immediately realise the implications for their land banks: instead of being a hoard for accumulating capital gains from rents created by others, they would become a financial liability. And so, anticipating the annual ground rent charge on their vacant sites, they would accelerate the output of new dwellings. This would stabilise house prices. Throughout Britain, ground rents would adjust to levels that people were willing and able to pay. These prospects would be mischievously represented as a "shock" in some sections of the media, foretelling the kinds of doom and gloom which were floated prior

---

Box 3:2 **The collateral benefits of AGR**

Land values are the narcotic to which the rent-seeking economy is addicted. Annual ground rents are capitalised and used as collateral for bank loans. By declaring the intention to replace taxes on earned incomes with AGR, the adjustments in financial behaviour would be swift. Banks would declare the plan a catastrophe: their capital base would be eroded by the loss of the value of land which they had taken as collateral from people who borrowed money.

• Government – and the banks – owe it to taxpayers to secure the transition to one similar to the German banking system, where lenders are more concerned with the ability of borrowers to repay the loans than with the lazy practise of settling for real estate as collateral.

In 2008, the financial sector seized up because of the toxic mortgages buried in bank vaults. Taxpayers were forced to carry the costs of reckless lending to housing markets across the US and Europe. Governments stepped in to rescue the banks.

To facilitate transition to AGR economics, banks should be comforted by the knowledge that borrowers would be even more reliable – in terms of paying back the loans – because real wages would rise as the Treadmill Taxes were removed.

• Home owners would need to be assured that the loss of that portion of their asset wealth which took the form of land value would not leave them vulnerable. Many people now rely on downsizing to raise cash to fund their care in old age. Transition arrangements would be needed to support them.

Home-owners would enjoy the concurrent reduction in taxes on wages and profits. They would invest in non-rent yielding assets. But some "capital rich/income poor" home owners might not be able to pay the AGR. Liability of AGR could be deferred until the house is sold, or out of the estate when the owner dies.

The net effect of the financial reform is that people would be better off than under the current fiscal regime. That is the copper-bottomed reason for everyone engaging in the business of making the reform work for the nation.

to the Brexit referendum. That is why careful preparation for the presentation of the policy is needed (see Box 3:2).

With these considerations in mind, the period of transition to the new fiscal system needs to be conflated into the shortest practical timetable. Acceleration of the pace of change would be driven by people who realised that the change-over would transform the status of land. As awareness of the implications fed into the public consciousness, the demand for change would flow from the bottom up. Abolishing the Treadmill Taxes would erase the anti-social status of land and rent, converting them into the pro-prosperity driving force which generates the growth that now eludes everyone but the richest 10% of asset owners.

Re-profiling the tax code

Which taxes to reduce first would be determined by circumstances prevailing in the economy.

▶ Boosting consumption, to stimulate output in the production of goods for the home market, would be achieved by a dramatic cut in VAT.

Mason Gaffney explains that the rewards would be huge. Across Europe, a revenue neutral strategy (one that maintained spending on existing services) which progressively diminished and then eliminated VAT would eventually leave EU citizens better off to the tune of about €1 trillion. Gaffney insists that this is a cautious calculation:

' To estimate the excess burdens of a tax like VAT as a trillion euros is a conservative estimate merely to open our minds to a vista of the society that can be – that we ourselves can create. To weight complex socio-economic phenomena in Euros, Pounds or Dollars necessarily poses a hazard of spurious precision and walled-in thinking. Who would presume to quantify the gains from synergy, or the losses from impeding it?'

Removing the "excess burden" of taxation would transform Europe beyond the current imagination. Conventional wisdom does not begin to articulate the prospects. What Gaffney calls "imagineering" is common coin in California's Silicon Valley – it connotes a more cosmic outlook than the concept of innovation – and he illustrated this phenomenon for me in these terms:

' The American social reformer Henry George attributed material progress to association in equality. Here is one of many living examples: who could have forecast the conversion of groves of prunes and apricots into the present Silicon Valley, or measured the gains of a novel industry based on a cheap, clean raw material, minimal capital, and abundant human brains and imagination, native and immigrant, arm in arm? One can assign no ceiling to human progress, once public policy lets and helps it happen, as by raising public revenues without excess burdens, and using the revenues to stimulate and free the minds and raise the hopes of the young and vigorous, and workers and "imagineering" of all ages.'

▶ Boosting employment would be achieved by reducing the Income Tax, which would induce employers to hire more workers.

Cutting taxes would need to take account of the prospect of attracting low-skilled workers from Eastern Europe during the time that the UK remained within the orbit of the EU's free movement of people. With 1.6m people in Britain unemployed in 2016 – a meaningless figure, when set against the 8.8m who were "economically inactive" (not working and not seeking or available to work) – the need for a new people-centred agenda is needed. Public services need more people working in prisons, in hospitals and schools, where there is a shortfall in qualified teachers. New forms of value adding activities are needed throughout the land, properly funded to enhance the wholesome lives of families and communities.

▶ Boosting capital formation would be achieved by abolishing Corporation Tax, which would attract foreign investment.

Funding "shovel-ready" small-scale infrastructure projects is a declared aim of Theresa May's Chancellor, Philip Hammond, who announced the intention to accelerate investment in road projects to raise productivity. By themselves, however, these public investments would also dislocate local economies, if the net gains are allowed to congeal in higher house prices. The risks from the sponge effect of tax cuts would be diminished if people became aware of the plan to phase in the Annual Ground Rent.

Threats from across the Channel

Two further considerations commend the need to institute tax reform without loss of time.

First, post-2008, the Eurozone failed to raise its growth rates to "escape velocity" levels. It remained dangerously close to a deflationary trap. Policy-makers were aware that they had exhausted monetary policy, and they had no supplementary tools with which to combat future shocks to the economy. A weakening Eurozone will accelerate the movement of migrants in the desperate search of work. If the Brexit negotiations become protracted, the UK would remain an attractive destination for low-skilled workers. The UK Government needs to publish a full audit of the impact of the European Union on the British economy and society. The benefits were emphasised by the Remainers during the Brexit referendum: an objective assessment of EU policies and practises needs to be provided, as much to alert the commissioners in Brussels on the scale of their own problems as to inform British citizens.

Second, the US and other countries warned that the UK would not be favoured with quick negotiations over new trade deals. And the EU's commissioners in Brussels signalled that they would push hard terms on the UK, if only to deter other member states from flirting with exit from the union.

Table 3:1 **Schedule for fiscal reform**		
	Government Initiatives	**Some Collateral Responses**
2016	Chancellor's Autumn Statement: announce review of all options on fiscal reform Theresa May orders publication of EU impact on UK	Cross-party discussions on priorities for Budget in the National Interest
2017	January: Theresa May announces audit of Treasury fiscal policies February: government triggers Article 50 March Budget: spending on front-line social services increased Autumn Statement: Outline of a "green" budget based on shift to AGR	Briefing Paper on EU problems stemming from its dysfunctional development model Housing sector energised
2018	March Budget: SME Investment Fund launched Publication of Report on Deadweight Losses from Taxes November Budget Statement: outline of new development model for trade with rest of the world based on free trade	Local authorities mandated to expand partnerships with house builders Cross-party Parliamentary agreement on fiscal reform
2019	People's Budget Mark II enacted: first cuts to taxes on lowest incomes Regional Development Bank announced, funds to be released in tandem with phased introduction of AGR	UK/EU agreement on trade Land valuation begins
2020	March Budget: Corporation Tax abolished Land value survey completed	General Election Phased introduction of AGR
2021	Income tax revenue cut by 50%, replaced by Annual Ground Rents	Full employment achieved

The threats from across the Channel make the expansion of the home market imperative for the UK. By accelerating the growth of domestically-produced and consumed goods and services, Britain would diminish the risks of being held hostage to the economic misfortunes of others. The only way to achieve a quantum leap in growth is by serving notice of plans for fiscal reform. Correctly explained by a government that was popularly perceived as knowing what it was doing, the confidence needed in the markets would generate the momentum towards the new economy. The AGR model would signal that the managerial ("fire-fighting") approach to administering the nation – of containing social crises and cramping personal ambitions – was being swapped for the creative role of enabling people to achieve their private and social potential. Based on these reflections, a schedule for the transition is shown in Table 3:1.

The Prime Minister should make an early announcement that the deadweight losses inflicted by government will be the subject of an independent enquiry.

With a tight majority of 16 in the House of Commons, and no majority in the Lords, Mrs May needs a popular mandate for her plans. An informal agreement between all the political parties on the wisdom of fiscal reform would be a practical start, of the kind that the Labour government could have formed with Churchill's Tories in 1945. Mrs May's recurring theme, building a new narrative for a rehabilitated democracy, would be developed around the concept of personal and institutional responsibility. Everyone, from those exercising power in government to the opposition parties and the electorate, needs to participate in renegotiating the social contract on honest fiscal foundations. To demonstrate leadership, the Prime Minister should make an early announcement that the deadweight losses inflicted by government will be the subject of an independent enquiry.

The logic for some of the foregoing initiatives becomes clear in the remainder of this blueprint. Future readers of Beyond Brexit will judge the outcome of Mrs May's first administration based on whether this schedule was adhered to, or not, and they will be able to accordingly attribute credit or blame.

The EU's art of social dumping

The European Union is out of political control under pressures from the rise of nationalism, the strengthening of regional breakup aspirations in Spain, Belgium, Italy and France, and the stresses imposed by Islamic fundamentalism and economic migration from Africa. Friction, not harmonisation, defines relationships between members. Brussels cannot hope for relief through an accelerated flow of job-hungry workers across the continent. In 2016 Austria and other member countries in the Balkans began to erect border barriers (ostensibly against refugees from the Middle East). There is now little likelihood of displacing social problems through the free movement of people.

Free migration is a non-negotiable condition of tariff-free access to the EU's single market. The policy ought to be called "social dumping", a term first employed by French Prime Minister Manuel Valls.[1] Social dumping has cost Britain's workers dearly. It forced the UK to import problems created elsewhere in Europe (see box).

Europe now finds itself back in the crisis of the early 1980s, when "eurosclerosis" was diagnosed. Social dumping was the solution.

The European Commission's strategies were outlined in a White Paper for the European Council that met in Milan in June 1985. Instead of removing the barriers to economic prosperity within each of the member countries, it chose the easy way out: accelerate the right of people to move. Border checks, it declared, were "the outward sign of an arbitrary administrative power over individuals and [...] an affront to the principle of freedom of movement within a single Community".[2]

By encouraging migration, relatively under-developed regions (which included swathes of Ireland, Portugal, Spain and Italy) were able to shift the costs of social welfare onto other countries. According to Valls, this caused "major, terrible damage in the world of workers, in industry". He explained that other EU countries "are not paying the same social charges and that cannot last, the social dumping is unbearable". France has one of Europe's most generous, and deeply indebted, social benefit systems.

But the dark clouds hanging over Europe today should not be blamed on migrants; nor can the threats to social stability be attributed to "globalisation". Chaos was prescribed by decisions taken in the 1950s. The architects of post-war Europe failed to match their aspirations with the form of governance that could secure both economic prosperity and social cohesion.

---

1 http://www.reuters.com/article/us-france-eu-workers-idUSKCN0ZJ0VD

2 European Commission (1985), *Completing the Internal Market*, Brussels, p.14, Para.48. http://europa.eu/documents/comm/white_papers/pdf/com1985_0310_f_en.pdf

More Jobs, Poorer Wages

The Cameron government claimed credit for the number of jobs created after 2008, but these came at a price. Average real hourly wages dropped by more than 10% between 2007 and 2015, according to OECD data analysed by the Trades Union Congress. France and the US enjoyed rising wages, but the price was greater unemployment. Germany alone achieved increases in employment and real wages.

With unemployment still above 10% across the EU in 2016, the movement of people in search of work was understandable. But in Britain's relatively unprotected labour market, that translated into a downward thrust in the bargaining power of employees, and a drop in the real value of wages.

The founding fathers wanted to banish the risk of another war. They drafted the European Convention on Human Rights in 1950. But the legal settlement was fatally flawed. By their acts of omission the statesmen permitted the reawakening of the financial parasite in the body politic that had lain dormant during the years of warfare. When re-aroused, that parasite would slowly but surely gnaw away at the European project. And so the fractures grew ever wider and more dangerous.

Europe's politicians deepened the *mentalité* that encourages perverse incentives and social stresses which, in the past, had led to territorial wars. And so, in response to Brexit and the risk of further fragmentation, the leaders of the EU's three largest countries - Germany, Italy and France - met on August 22, 2016, on the island of Ventotene, 30 miles from Naples. The meeting was supposed to be a symbolic affirmation of unity.

One of the architects of the plan for a federal European state was Altiero Spinelli, an Italian communist who was imprisoned on the island during World War 2. In his cell, using language derived from Marx and 19th century socialists, he crafted his "manifesto" for Europe. One proposal was that the constitution would be created *after* the main political and administrative institutions, and the power they would wield, had been established. So the power structure was hard-wired into the system first, and only then were member governments invited to consider the terms of a constitution.

The correct approach would have been an open-minded conversation on how to establish a modern industrial (or post-industrial) society from scratch. Instead, the statesmen assumed they knew the correct parameters for the European project.

They didn't.

Given the devastated state of Europe in the early years after the world war, one sensible approach would have been to ask themselves: *How, under these conditions of duress, should we set about building the best social system possible?* This was the question that European colonists had asked themselves when they landed in territories like Australia, New Zealand, Argentina and South Africa. Infrastructure and the enterprise economy had to be built from scratch. How would they fund the development of those territories? There was one sensible answer only: out of ground rents! Their remarkable success was achieved with virtually no aid from outside.

4

Dealing with the EU

THE FATE of the UK and the nations of Europe will forever remain interwoven. In transforming the UK into an inclusive society, it is in Britain's interest to enhance the welfare of the countries that remain in the EU. Even if the EU cannot claim the credit for preserving peace in Europe - the absence of conflict had more to do with NATO, the Cold War and the fear of mutual destruction - its participation in the quest for peaceful co-existence remains paramount.

The opportunity for the EU to pause in its headlong rush into a federal state, and take stock, was a gift from the people of Britain who voted for Brexit. There was no recognition of this as the prime ministers and presidents of the 27 remaining members of the EU gathered in a castle in Slovakia on September 16, 2016, to draft a roadmap into the future. Responsibility fell on them for the many stresses that were threatening the union, but they were not prepared to accept personal responsibility. Instead, they preferred to shift guilt to impersonal forces like "globalisation". Their Bratislava Declaration ordered the civil servants in Brussels to conjure up a rescue plan, to be delivered when they reconvened in Rome in March 2017 to celebrate the signing of the Treaty of Rome 60 years earlier in 1957.

The inquest into Europe's problems provided the citizens of the 27 member nations with a unique opportunity to reconstitute the union. The UK was entitled to contribute to this inquest, in the form of a debriefing paper on why the majority of voters favoured Brexit. That appraisal of the customs and practices of the EU could be used constructively to reshape the union's future. If the UK and the EU engaged in good faith, it would be possible to establish a new social *milieu* that enhanced relationships throughout Europe. That outcome, however, was conditional on an honest exploration into the way the EU affects people's lives. Understanding the proximate causes of the chaos which disturbs the continent is achieved by working backwards in time.

The fault lines within the EU reveal what was missing from the attempt to create harmony across the continent. The major error was in failing to align fiscal policy to sustain a common monetary policy. The EU and its common currency, the euro, had to rely on policies administered by the central bank in Frankfurt. Interest rates were standardised across the economic space. But without centralised political power over the fiscal system, disaster was inevitable.

The arrangements favoured Germany. The low interest rate regime stimulated fixed capital formation and led to a huge trade surplus created by Germany's exporting enterprises. Elsewhere, however, low interest rates had a corrosive effect: easy credit fuelled land speculation, which disrupted countries along the southern rim, the arc stretching from Cyprus through the Mediterranean to Ireland. The peripheral regions ran trade deficits and built unsustainable debts. This was an avoidable disaster. The incoherence in macro-economic policy was anticipated in 1992 (see Box 4:1).

Box 4:1 **The fatal omission of fiscal policy**

Economist Wynne Godley, who served in the UK's Treasury before moving to the University of Cambridge, diagnosed with precision the prospects of the euro experiment. He warned that, without the support of a tax system that could redistribute income, regional economies would be savagely damaged by a common currency. Membership of the free market did not offer protection from the forces that sucked resources away from peripheral regions into the centre of power. Wynne Godley warned:

' If a country or region has no power to devalue, and if it is not the beneficiary of a system of fiscal equalisation, then there is nothing to stop it suffering a process of cumulative and terminal decline leading, in the end, to emigration as the only alternative to poverty or starvation.' *

That is a forensic description with special resonance for countries like Greece, Ireland, Spain and Portugal. Britain avoided the risks by opting not to join the Euro.

* Wynne Godley (1992), "Maastricht and All That", *London Review of Books*, Vol. 14(19), October 8.

The impact of incoherent economic policies on people's lives resulted in the fleeing of millions of workers from the southern and eastern regions. With the closing of the UK border imminent, the stresses on labour markets within the Eurozone will intensify as economic migrants concentrate in fewer hotspots in the central growth zones. In the UK, the number of migrant workers from Eastern Europe alone passed the one million mark in June 2016. This included a 16% increase in Bulgarians and Romanians after migration controls in their countries were lifted in January 2014. For the exporting countries, the haemorrhaging of able-bodied workers entailed the loss of wealth that would have been produced within their communities if the EU had favoured balanced economic development in all communities throughout the union.

Following the 2008 crisis, attempts to stabilise the EU economy proved a lamentable failure. By failing to deploy the correct fiscal policy as one tool for

---

Box 4:2 **Sclerosis in Euroland**

The EU has come to terms with harsh reality: stagnation is the "new normal". Between 2008 and 2016, aggregate Eurozone real gross domestic product rose by a trivial 0.5%, while real aggregate demand fell by 2.4%. Real GDP per capita was forecast to rise 11% in Germany, stagnate in France and fall by 8% (Spain) and 11% (Italy). Unemployment among young people achieved rates of up to 50% in some peripheral regions.

In Greece, the economy continued into freefall despite multi-billion dollar "rescue" packages. Joseph Stiglitz ruminated on the motives of the Troika.

'[T]he Troika could have pushed for the progressive property tax aimed at the oligarchs...rather than the tax they insisted upon, a non-progressive one that hurt so many who were already suffering so much. Such a comprehensive and progressive property tax would, of course, have been resisted by the oligarchs who own so much of Greece's wealth, and that makes it precisely the kind of issue on which the Troika should have weighed in.'

Utterly perplexed, Stiglitz was moved to suggest sinister motives:

'[A]s one looked at the details of the Troika programs, one wondered what side the Troika was on: Was it just an accident, a slip, that they opted for a property tax that would have inflicted pain on ordinary Greeks, rather than one that would have hit the oligarchs?' *

* Joseph Stiglitz (2016) *The Euro and its Threat to the Future of Europe*, London: Penguin, p.227.

---

rebuilding the economy, the dogmas championed by the Troika – the IMF, Brussels and the European Central Bank – erupted as "austerity" measures. The pain endured in Greece exposed a vicious approach to healing reminiscent of the medieval doctor's blood-letting practise of severing a patient's arteries to effect a cure. Needless to say, the cure failed (see Box 4:2).

The EU favoured the Value Added Tax. But this instrument could not be sensibly deployed to raise spending power and consumer confidence in a time of recession. On the contrary: raising VAT rates would drive down the spending in shops, while cutting VAT rates would expose governments to ever larger budgetary deficits. Standard economic theory could have alerted the statesmen who harboured the desire to transform Europe from a common market into a political federation. If governance was to be benign and democratic, it would have to feature the hallmarks of openness and accountability. Instead, they favoured the duplicity on which modern tax policy is based. That duplicity was analysed by two British civil servants who worked as Information Officers for the European Community in the 1960s. At the time, Britain was debating whether to join the Common Market.

Roger Broad and Robert Jarrett published an assessment of how European institutions operated. On the issue of revenue, they noted that there was a problem with direct taxes such as income tax and social security contributions – "the citizen is immediately aware of how much is being deducted from their pay-packet". How could the pan-European institutions overcome this awkward problem of transparency? "If much tax is raised indirectly (e.g. through purchase or sales taxes), the citizen is less aware of how much tax he is paying…" That need for deception pointed to VAT as the tool for funding the Brussels-based institutions. The outcome is distortions to personal behaviour and the macro-economy. Broad and Jarrett were at least honest about the dishonesty of a fiscal system that seeks to covertly extract revenue from people.[1]

The civil servants in Brussels who wrote the position papers and draft treaties for governments to ratify were skilled in using language which deceived. They rationalised their plans around the claim that they wanted to eliminate distortions in the marketplace. Their mantra was *harmonisation*. And yet, by choosing the regressive VAT as its tax of choice, the EU imposed the greatest burdens on the people with the lowest incomes. Far from facilitating the free movement of goods and services to optimise welfare, VAT reinforced the other distortions – financial and regulatory – inflicted by Brussels. The outcome was the weakened economy which plunged unprotected into the financial storms of 2008. That model of High Finance was rationalised as the pursuit of "freedom".

The legacy of Rome

The EU hypes its Four Freedoms – movement of people, capital, goods and services – as the cornerstone of its model of peace and prosperity. That was a false promise from the start, and the euro gave the lie to the claim. Again, an objective assessment of the evidence would have alerted the founding fathers of the European project to the dangers of a flawed social contract. The dynamics of cross-border economics combined with centralised power have been on the record in Europe for 2,000 years. The social pathologies associated with such a combination reveal themselves in the financial system. They were incubated in the time of Jesus, as a direct consequence of the earliest treaties concocted in Rome.

When power is unequally distributed, rent is sucked into the political centre – the heartland of privilege. That process operates at all levels of economic engagement:

▶ between a city and its agricultural hinterland

▶ within a region

▶ across a sovereign state, or

▶ spanning a continent united by an unenlightened authority.

That model emerged across Europe two millennia ago when Rome constructed roads north, south, east and west to build its empire. Tribes were pacified, and the economic outcome was revealed in the statistics compiled

---

1 Roger Broad and Robert Jarrett (1967), *Community Europe*, London: Oswald Wolff, p.54.

Table 4:1 **Ancient Rome and modern Europe**	
A Rents and the Treaties of Rome (14 AD)		**B** GDP for selected European countries (2015: estimate)
	Per capita income 1990 G-K $	*Per capita* income (purchasing power parity) US $
Italy	809	35,700
France	473	41,200
Belgium	450	43,600
Germany	408	46,900
Denmark	400	45,700
Source: Maddison (2007), Table 1.13, p.56.		Source: CIA Factbook https://www.cia.gov/library/publi-cations/the-world-factbook/docs/profileguide.html

by Angus Maddison (1926–2010), the British economist who specialised in quantitative macroeconomic history.

Maddison estimated the distribution of income in 14 AD. To reveal the spatial logic at work in the way income was distributed, we may draw a cross-section from Rome in any of the directions of the compass. The data for one line, drawn north-westwards across the European heartland, is show in Column A of Table 4:1. This reveals the income disparities along the Roman roads as far as Denmark. Entered on a graph, the values reveal the classic Ricardian rent profile: highest at the centre and sloping downwards to the furthest point of the empire, the outer region which (as described in David Ricardo's theoretical model) was the economic margin. If the Danes could live on $400, half the income in Italy was rent.

Variations in gross value added *per capita* cannot be attributed to greater skills of people working in and around Rome. They were all to do with what I elsewhere call the predator culture.[2] Maddison left his readers in no doubt about what drove the differences in *per capita* incomes.

' Much bigger gains came from acquisition of provinces outside the peninsula. This led to an inflow of booty and slaves on a very large scale and allowed the elite to acquire large property holdings and rental income outside the peninsula…The inflow of slaves meant that labour input per head of population in peninsular Italy was proportionately much higher than in the provinces. A more intensive use of

2 Fred Harrison (2010), *The Predator Culture: The Systemic Roots and Intent of Organised Violence*, London: Shepheard-Walwyn.

agricultural land with slave labour and the large inflow of tribute wheat made it possible to increase specialisation of agricultural output. Peninsular Italy also had a better infrastructure of roads and ports than the rest of the empire. The main beneficiaries of this transformation and growth were the elite group.'[3]

This imperial history can be summed up in a simple economic sequence in which land owners

1. extracted rents from outer regions
2. invested in Rome's highway infrastructure
3. drove down labour costs
4. raised output on plantations
5. captured increased revenue as rent

The collateral consequence was the impoverishment of the outer regions. That outcome is inevitable when the net income is not shared equitably among everyone in all parts of the economy.

The architects of the European Union turned a blind eye on this lesson of history. They did so, even though a rigorous analysis of the economic process at work was published by a distinguished Oxford economist. In 1969, Colin Clark demonstrated theoretically that the European Economic Community (EEC) would be divided into an inner rich region, and an impoverished outer periphery. He arrived at his conclusion by using location theory. This highlights the way in which rents emerge in response to lower transport costs. Clark explained that Germany had the advantage of location in modern Europe. That advantage would be exploited to the full within the EEC at the expense of the southern rim of Europe. He and his co-authors provided maps to demonstrate the gradient – the downward slope on the graph. And they provided a clear warning of what would happen in the labour market.

' [T]he possibility arises that the labour and capital of Common Market countries which are remote from the potential centre of Europe will migrate to the centre, to the detriment of the countries on the periphery.' [4]

This prognosis was to be confirmed by events which unfolded across Europe, as illustrated by the data in Column B of Table 4:1. Resources were shifted to the centre, at the expense of the peripheral countries. Today, Germany tops the income league, closely followed by Denmark, far outstripping the other countries in *per capita* income. *The spatial profile that prevailed in the time of Jesus remained, but the tables were turned on Rome!* If harmonisation was to be the guiding ethos, rather than exploitation, this could only be achieved by pooling and sharing the continent's net income.

---

3 Angus Maddison (2007), *Contours of the World Economy, 1-2030AD*, Oxford: Oxford University Press, p.56. Maddison explains (on p.298) the methodology for estimating incomes in the time of Jesus: the method was invented by Roy Geary (1896-1983) and Salem Khamis (1919-2005), hence the G-K notation.
4 C. Clark, F. Wilson and J. Bradbury (1969), *Location and Economic Potential in Western Europe*, Oxford: Agricultural Economics Research Institute, April, p.208.

By ignoring the financial impact of the original treaties that Rome imposed on the tribes of Europe, the statesmen who signed the Treaty of Rome in 1957 (to create the EEC) authorised the economics of apartheid. Europe would be systematically divided into rich and poor regions, and would operate to the advantage of the rent-seekers.

The fiscal divide

Critics of the euro argue that the flaw with Europe's common currency was the failure to align it with a robust fiscal system. That is not the whole truth. Sterling unites the UK's four nations, and the dollar unites the 50 states of America: and they operate alongside powerful tax regimes. Yet, both the UK and the USA are divided by the same mechanism that operated in 14 AD.[5] Income redistribution aided by Treadmill Taxes does not inoculate populations against the epidemic that was incubated in Rome and circulated across Europe!

> The mechanism that provides automatic stabilisation is the fiscal system that draws revenue from Annual Ground Rents to fund public services across the economic space.

The mechanism that provides automatic stabilisation is the fiscal system that draws revenue from Annual Ground Rents to fund public services across the economic space. That policy nurtures all communities and forestalls the land-led booms and busts which periodically disrupt the economy. By ignoring this reality, governments of the EU's 28 member states deprived their populations of wealth and welfare of at least €1 trillion in 2015, attributable to VAT alone. This does not include the losses created by all the other taxes. The deadweight losses include the damage caused by EU budget-funded corruption, and the waste of resources entailed in complying with the complex regulatory system. Those losses would not have been incurred if the EU had retired the Treadmill Taxes in favour of revenue from AGR. Instead, by conforming to the fiscal legacy of the feudal aristocracy, the EU made itself responsible for the ensuing chaos. This included the damage caused by the uncontrolled movement of people, which helped to drive up the costs of housing, drive down wages of low-income workers and intensify the social stresses that led to Brexit.

The estimate of a €1 trillion net gain from abolishing VAT within Europe is based on transforming the conditions which exist today. But try to imagine the

---

5 For a detailed examination of the spatial process as it is played out in the UK, see Fred Harrison (2006), *Ricardo's Law*, London: Shepheard-Walwyn.

state of affairs if Europe's governments had instituted the AGR funding model during the formative years of the European project. Such a hypothesis is not fantasy. As we saw in Chapter 2, Denmark in the 1950s laid the foundations for a dynamic economy on the back of the AGR funding policy. European governments could have drawn on that lesson. The gravitational pull towards the Danish model would have enhanced economic prosperity by gains measured in the hundreds of billions of francs, Deutschemarks and all the other currencies then existing – year in, year out, and benefitting from the magic of a *virtuous* compound interest!

But we need not rely exclusively on history for deducing the benefits to Europe of the AGR model.

When Estonia secured freedom from the Soviet Union in 1991, she came away with a poor dowry: an economy that had been suppressed by Soviet central planning. The Estonians modernised their constitution. For municipal finance, they opted for the AGR model. Professionals from Denmark were called in. Land was valued separately from buildings, and the new fiscal system was established in double-quick time. Then, when Estonia joined the EU in 2004, her aim was to catch up with her richer neighbours. The achievements have been remarkable. According to the Heritage Foundation's Index of Economic Freedom 2016, "Estonia is one of the world's most dynamic and modern economies and has the EU's lowest debt-to-GDP ratio".[6] The CIA Factbook reported Estonia's GDP *per capita* in 2015 as $28,600, outstripping Portugal's $27,800 and Greece's $26,400 (comparisons in terms of purchasing power parity).

The land tax in Estonia is not comprehensive. It is correctly levied on the value of land alone, but the rate is low. The revenues are devoted exclusively to funding municipal needs. Edward Lucas, an editor at *The Economist*, argues that "Estonia could look into making more of the land tax system, which would be progressive and fair".[7] But as a member of the EU, Estonia cannot replace VAT with AGR. Even so, her investment rates and speed of redevelopment testify to the influence of a fiscal reform that is accelerating the renewal of this north-eastern corner of Europe.

The empirical evidence from Denmark and Estonia is waiting to be scrutinised by the commissioners in Brussels, so that the news may be circulated throughout the continent. Would Brussels benefit from a nudge from London?

Article 50

The process for UK withdrawal from the EU is defined in Article 50 of the Lisbon Treaty. A new agreement based on the EU's present practices is not possible, if the May government is determined to rebalance the British economy

---

6 http://www.heritage.org/index/country/estonia
7 http://estonianworld.com/life/edward-lucas-estonia-is-now-an-insider-not-an-outsider-anymore-an-interview-with-the-economists-international-editor/

and society. The biggest single obstacle to a free trade deal is the free movement of people. Britain's negotiators need to arm themselves with a narrative which encompasses the doctrine of freedom of people to move, but one which exercises the moral force that might enable the EU to abandon its dogma of unfettered movement. The terms of such a narrative can be constructed to serve everyone's best interests.

The EU justifies its notion of labour mobility with the word *freedom*. That freedom is said to be with a purpose: harmonize everyone's interests by overriding barriers to prosperity. As applied, however, the doctrine is dishonest.

The harmonic qualities of the EU's notion of freedom in relation to the right to work can be rigorously tested by asking two questions.

1. Are EU member governments willing to employ practices which guarantee the freedom of their citizens to remain in their home communities?

Countries offend the principle of freedom if they enforce practices which result in people being driven out of their homeland in search of work. Those countries should be disqualified from being parties to an agreement that facilitated the unchecked movement of people across national borders. None of the Eurozone countries meets this standard of freedom (except Germany and Denmark?). The UK, in its Article 50 negotiations, ought to argue that free movement should be suspended until tax policies are amended to secure people's freedom to remain in their home communities.

2. Are economic migrants welcomed on the basis of mutual benefit for both host and the people-exporting countries?

An efficient migration policy maximises the welfare of the migrant and the taxable income of the recipient country, without impoverishing the exporting country. This outcome does not prevail in Europe today. Colin Clark was correct to emphasise that countries on the periphery would be impoverished by the loss of productive workers.

Both the EU and the UK would gain from an agreement grounded, first and foremost, in a development model that empowered citizens to live and work in the place of their birth. Such a partnership would have to be underpinned by strict criteria for determining whether individual countries were, indeed, applying the principles of freedom. The terms for such an arrangement include

▶ *free trade:* no State may exploit a neighbour by retaining barriers that distort the production and exchange of goods and services, including distortions in labour markets; and

▶ *fiscal policies:* no State may distort their economies with policies which (as happens today) disrupt communities (such as fishing villages) and productive sectors (such as agriculture).

The European Commission would have to revise the treaties and policies that underpin the EU. The UK would also have to admit that its social model is defective. Throughout Britain's regions, young people are forced to move in search of work because of the arbitrary barriers to employment in their home communities. By conforming to the principles of a new Freedom Deal, migration would of its own accord be confined to levels that met the needs of communities and nations that exported its people, and met the needs of nations that received migrants into their communities. The outcome would be a balanced relationship between the UK and the EU. Economic development across the continent would be accelerated, as measured by the increase in net income. The pan-European share-out of rents would far exceed what is being allocated today as VAT-funded subsidies to maintain the peripheral regions in their poverty-stricken state.

With such an agreement in place, the UK and the EU could conclude a free trade deal that excluded tariff barriers.

Britain's trump cards

The UK has been presented with a unique dialectical opportunity. By setting an example, it could animate a new ethos for Europe.

Britain's negotiating position would be enhanced if Theresa May's government could mobilise a political coalition behind the AGR model within Westminster. AGR (in a weak form) is already endorsed by some Labour and Liberal Party leaders, and it is enshrined in the Green Party's manifesto. Theresa May would discover she was pushing against an open door in Parliament. The vision to achieve consensus behind fiscal reform would be that of a new partnership between government and the people.

But nothing is to be gained by underplaying the difficulties in reaching a Win-Win agreement with the EU. The resentment harboured against the UK by commissioners in Brussels is not disguised. Nonetheless, the UK holds the trump cards. The three biggest EU economies are net beneficiaries of trade with the UK. Germany, France and Italy export more to British consumers than they buy from British exporters. It is in their economic interest to control the mood in Brussels.

Brussels, however, may choose to call the UK's bluff in the Article 50 negotiations. There is one way to check-mate that strategy. The UK can position itself so that, even if exports were curtailed by unfavourable tariff terms, the British economy would not suffer. How could this be achieved? The AGR economy would expand the size of the UK market by more than what might be lost in trade with Europe. *UK producers would have their hands full meeting domestic demand!*

If the UK and the EU agree on the need to rebalance their systems, they would have discovered the Holy Grail in economics. The mechanism that

Box 4:3 **The EU Homeland Charter**

The distress-driven displacement of people from their home communities is used by the EU as the cruel tool for automatically stabilising the economy. It has not worked. Despite the millions who have been forced to traverse the continent in search of work, the Eurozone continues to suffer high levels of regional unemployment.

Instead of addressing their problems, EU leaders hostile to Britain warn that the City of London will lose its "passports" – the free access that financiers enjoy to make money out of money in Europe. The "passports" held by UK firms total over 330,000, with 23,000 held by EU businesses. But where are the "passport" privileges for people who are denied the freedom to remain and work in their place of birth, where they may wish to start a family in a home of their own? They are driven out by the want of work opportunities.

The net outcome needs to be calculated. One measure was noted by the OECD. It warns that large-scale movement is not correctly monitored in the localities settled by displaced people from regions like the Balkans. Problems as they affect the labour and housing markets, and municipal budgets, are ignored by national governments. The net effect is measured in the property market. While immigration of high earners "tends to lead to an increase of the average level of local rents...the opposite seems to be the case when immigrants are poor".[1]

The OECD warns that "a low-growth trap has taken root, as poor growth expectations further depress trade, investment, productivity and wages", but it fails to identify innovative policies which would divert the global economy from "cardiac arrest".[2]

If the EU wishes to escape the low-growth trap, and if it wishes to guarantee the freedom of everyone to work, it must enact a Homeland Charter. This must guarantee people's right to work in the communities of their birth by outlawing the barriers to prosperity enforced by the State. The humane automatic stabilisation mechanism is based on a public revenue system which democratises power and holds governments to account for their actions.

1 OECD (2016), *Migration Outlook 2016*, Paris, p. 134.
2 David Haugh *et al* (2016), *Cardiac Arrest or Dizzy Spell*, Paris: OECD Economic Policy Paper No. 18.

balances the economy *and society* ensures that metropolitan centres do not inflate to monstrous levels of inefficiency. Regional growth centres would develop in harmony with communities in their hinterland. Through spending on public services, no-one would be excluded from a direct share of the net benefits. Europe would have unlocked the secret of sustainable economics, healthy communities and happy citizens.

The open economy grounded in the principles of fiscal justice would electrify communities throughout the continent. There would be an automatic shift towards

▶ reskilling of unemployed and under-employed workers, in response to the needs of investors creating new enterprises. Productivity would be raised, with the manufacturing and service sectors expanded within each country, reducing the need for out- migration. And

▶ reduced trade deficits between the UK and EU, and between members within the EU, with total output increased to generate higher *per capita* living standards. Improved productivity would enhance European competitiveness and open up new global markets for exports.

At the Bratislava conclave, European Council president Donald Tusk called for "brutal honesty" in appraising the crises that challenge Europe. But when the politicians saw the word "chaos" in the draft of their Declaration, placed there to describe the migration crisis, honesty was sacrificed in favour of diplomacy. The word was deleted.[8] The peoples of Europe are entitled to nothing less than brutal honesty. The UK Government has the honour of delivering the full and frank appraisal of what is at stake. One initiative would be for Britain to draft – as a parting gift – the terms of an EU Homeland Charter (see Box 4:3).

---

8 Alex Barker *et al* (2016), "EU leaders focus on bonhomie and put off tough decisions", *Financial Times*, 17 September.

Putting up with anti-social behaviour

Joseph Stiglitz addresses the lopsided nature of capitalism with proposals for re-writing the rules of the economy. New regulatory regimes and a hardening of anti-trust laws, to augment tax reform, are intended to prevent corporations from exploiting consumers and government.[1] But viewed in terms of social psychology, serious problems arise when governments favour regulation rather than shifting taxes off wages and onto rents. By failing to remove the rewards sought by rent-seekers, governments implicitly resign themselves to living with an ethos based on the unremitting search for ways to bend the rules.

By devoting resources to fine-tuning regulatory systems, a government confesses that it accepts the reality of anti-social behaviour and will settle for trying to tame the worst excesses. The tolerated levels of anti-social behaviour are determined not by principle, but by political horse-trading. This cultivates the rent-seeking behaviour by nurturing the "chance-your-luck" culture. Lawyers and accountants are employed to figure out if the rules can be bent for profit. The systemic shortcomings in the regulatory approach were revealed by the failure, following the 2008 banking crisis, to identify strategies that could prevent Wall Street and the City of London from funding the next property boom/bust crisis.

The forensic solution is fiscal. By collecting rents to fund public services, behaviour is changed in favour of seeking competitive rewards by providing goods and services for which customers are willing to pay. Monopoly power disappears. People behave responsibly and corporations settle for a competitive return on their investments.

This is not to say that all regulations and bureaucratic oversight should be abolished (the dream of American libertarians). It does mean that, insofar as governments are not willing to use fiscal tools to remove the temptation to grab any part of the nation's net income, someone needs to be held accountable. Meanwhile, society suffers from the costs of administering complex regulatory systems. These sometimes evolved into Kafkaesque confrontations. Such was the case in 2015. During his budget speech, Britain's Chancellor of the Exchequer, George Osborne, warned employees that they could expect to be taxed on wages they did not receive.

- The taxman had discovered that firms were providing benefits to employees (such as cell phones and laptops) in return for lower salaries. The so-called salary sacrifice schemes enabled people to swap chunks of their salary for non-taxable perks, which reduced revenue to the taxman.

---

1 Joseph Stiglitz (2016), *Rewriting the Rules of the American Economy*, New York: Roosevelt Institute.

The regulatory approach to policing rent-seeking behaviour requires armies of civil servants to administer complex rules. These rules are manipulated by corporate lawyers in the search for loopholes, which consequently requires yet more rules to plug the holes. Policy-making time is consumed by the search for palliatives to address the latest crises created by the rule-benders.

- Mike Basman is not a corporate tax-dodger. As a volunteer, he organises the world's biggest chess contest for children. The taxman decided that he should have collected Value Added Tax from schools that entered children in the competition. A tax bill for £300,000 bankrupted Basman, who faced the prospect of losing his home.

Mike Basman explained the absurdity of the rules: "If I collect this VAT, I have to fill out endless forms and hire accountants, and then the schools just claim it back from the taxman anyway".[2]

The regulatory apparatus is administered by civil servants funded out of the taxes that constrain productivity and which discriminate in favour of rent-seekers. Government now has to compress public services to accommodate the erosion of revenues as productivity declines. The decline of the Welfare State is overseen by civil servants who enjoy fabulous salaries and gold-plated pensions. According to media reports, some of their departments are riddled with allegations of gross inefficiency and corruption.

- Over 700 civil servants, officials and "quangocrats" earned more than £100,000 in 2015, according to analysis of official figures by The Daily

Telegraph. The number earning more than the Prime Minister's £142,500 salary had risen to 332, with the highest earner paid £750,000.[3]

Some of those officials work for the NHS, which in 2016 faced the prospect of the closure of hospitals to overcome a £460m funding shortfall. Many patients have lost their lives in NHS hospitals due to administrative failures.

The social costs of the regulatory approach to containing rent-seeking behaviour need to be calculated. Without an estimate of those costs, policy-makers cannot be held accountable by their constituents.

Do the losers have a case for compensation? Unlike the corporations and high net worth individuals, they lack the power to lobby government for the privileged treatment that gives access to the rents which are allowed to seep through the regulatory net. If society claims to honour the principle of equal treatment, why should the losers endure a net loss? Equity requires that those who profit from the residual monopoly power tolerated by the State should compensate the losers. What would be an appropriate rate of compensation? A sum equal to the benefits of monopoly power? But in that case, what would be the point in exercising monopoly power?

---

2 Leon Watson (2016), "World's biggest chess contest under threat in row with taxman", Daily Telegraph, August 29.

3 http://www.telegraph.co.uk/news/2016/08/29/more-than-700-civil-servants-officials-and-quangocrats-earned-mo/

5

Does it add up?

THE DUKE of Westminster's death was awkwardly timed for Prime Minister Theresa May. An estate estimated to be worth between £8bn and £9bn was left to his 25-year-old bachelor son, Hugh. The Grosvenor estate included 100 acres of Mayfair and 200 acres of Belgravia – some of the most expensive real estate on earth. But the inheritance tax would be trivial: most of the assets were held in trusts.

The "silver spoon" story of the duke's son is a direct challenge to the philosophy that the Prime Minister promised to turn into legislative action. In her first power-talk with the owners of small and medium sized businesses who gathered in Downing Street on August 4, 2016, Mrs May declared her goal: "an economy balanced across the UK and open to new opportunities". But that balance could not be achieved without challenging doctrines on wealth and the rights of property.

Right-wing ideologues leapt into action. They warned Mrs May to avoid policies wreathed around the notion of equality. One of them, Charles Moore, the authorised biographer of Margaret Thatcher, insisted: "Most wealth creation works to the general good, but one of its inevitable consequences is that some people do a lot better than others. This helps provide an index of what works and what doesn't".[1] That assertion, deployed to defend a £9bn fortune, summed up the political dilemma for a reformist politician. For when rent-based wealth is privately accumulated it is not an indicator of what works. Land owners are gatekeepers who extract rent from those who need access either to nature's resources or society's services (or both). Rent is a pure transfer income.

Go far enough back in history, and we see that the pedigree of the current system of land tenure is pillage. This was followed by the hijacking of political power and the transformation of natural law into the legislation which rationalises the hoards accumulated by the land grabbers of old. Hugh Richard Louis Grosvenor, the new Duke of Westminster, is the beneficiary of that history. His father – an honest and modest man – did not seek to deny that fact.

---

1 Charles Moore (2016), "A duke's wealth is the natural result of a free society – and should be celebrated", *Daily Telegraph*, August 13.

Box 5:1 **Cashing in on leaseholds, Grosvenor-style**

According to the London *Evening Standard*, the Grosvenor Estate will only grant leases for up to 20 years on its properties. This makes good business sense, as was illustrated in the case of an apartment at No1 Eaton Square. It was to be auctioned in 2016 for a guide price of £295,000, with just 22 months left on the lease. When the lease expires, the leaseholder would be free to buy a further lease of 20 years on payment to Grosvenor of what was expected to be £500,000 to £600,000.* The leasehold payment would be pure land rent, because the building had long ago paid for itself (amortisation), and upkeep is covered by service charges paid by leaseholders. The new duke will not have created the £500,000 value that his estate will pocket when the lease in Eaton Square is renewed. That value is pure annual ground rent, capitalised and paid up-front to the estate.

* Mira Bar-Hillel and Jonathan Prym (2016), "Buy a flat in James Bond's square for less than a des res in Dagenham", Evening Standard, August 15.

The problem, however, is not with today's landlords, but with governance that sanctions the perpetuation of the crimes of the past. Those crimes are inflicted on a daily basis in every street and city. And that is why the Welfare State is prevented from equalising people's life chances (see Box 4:1).

The Single Tax

To reinforce the moral imperatives on which this blueprint is based, statistics are offered as measures of the damage inflicted by taxes. This is intended to encourage reflection on the scale of what can be achieved by the abolition of Treadmill Taxes. But statistics need to be handled with caution. The classical philosophers described how government could and should be funded out of rent. That policy was known in the 19th century as the Single Tax. Today, reports Joseph Stiglitz, "Most economists would say that you cannot run the US economy on the 'Single Tax'".[2] The pessimism on which those economists base that assertion stems from their failure to approach the public's finances in a comprehensive and objective manner.

The starting point for the re-appraisal of taxation is the realisation that All *current* Taxes Come Out of Rent (ATCOR). This thesis, in its modern elucidation, and with its qualifications, is explored by economists, lawyers, land owners and property professionals in *Rent Unmasked*. The clarity needed to realise that current taxes are, ultimately, at the expense of rents, was undermined by the post-classical economists who shredded the distinction between public and private realities. The lamentable failure to address the realities of how national income is distributed under the influence of fiscal

---

2 Christopher Williams (2003), "Redefining the Washington Consensus: An interview with Joseph Stiglitz", Geophilos, Vol. 3 (1), p.53.

policy is understandable. If the Single Tax theory is practical economics, most of the current economic doctrines as they relate to politics would be rendered obsolete.

The major difficulty with the AGR model of public finance is not with computation. Land owners, building companies, and speculators calculate the future flows of rents from parcels of land on a daily basis. Rather, it is the psychological challenge of appreciating that the human personality is a synthesis of two realms – private and social – and that this complexity can be expressed in statistical values that accurately reflect economic reality. For ideological reasons, in the 20th century it was not in the interests of the Left or the Right to apply that reality to the formulation of public policy.

▶ After 1945, socialists emphasised nationalisation, transgressing the private domain in a crude blunderbuss attempt to solve the injustices of capitalism.

▶ Libertarians countered with privatisation, transgressing the public domain in a crude philosophical attempt to defend the *status quo*.

Ideological warfare banished from the collective consciousness the classical concepts which distinguished the public sphere from the private realm. The consequence is chaos in the domain of politics.

The risks in numbers

Politicians employ statistics in place of rigorous thought. This has the convenient effect of distracting people from the ethical implications of decisions made in their name. Hard numbers imply a precision that is often spurious. But bogus statistics influence the making of policies which fail to deliver the desired outcomes. That was illustrated by the data on the output of housing in Britain. In response to the low rate of completion of new dwellings, the Cameron Government provided tax-funded incentives to bump up the rate of production and purchase of new houses. But that policy was calibrated to numbers which seriously under-estimated the output of new dwellings.[3]

With these reflections in mind, we need to consider the statistics used to reveal the order-of-magnitude of the shortfall in incomes stemming from Treadmill Taxes. My numbers are offered, bearing in mind the stricture attributed to Albert Einstein: "Not everything that can be counted counts, and not everything that counts can be counted".

It is not possible to capture in a single number all of the gains from fiscal reform. When the economy is free to flourish, the ensuing benefits are constantly fructifying. Some of these gains cannot be quantified (see Box 5:2).

Nevertheless, statistics are needed to arouse the collective imagination and stimulate debate about the need for reform. That conversation has already started

---

3 Kate Allen (2016), "One in five new homes missing from England's official data", *Financial Times*, Sept.19.

Box 5:2 **The problem with 'hard' numbers**

Reducing complex behaviour to a few hard numbers runs the risk of playing the game of those who dissemble with reality; not least, by over-complicating the issues, deploying arbitrary assumptions and ordaining obscure rules of accounting. One ruse is the Capital Gains Game. This involves converting an annual stream of income (rent) into capital gains, and then denying (for tax purposes) that capital gains are really income. This ring-fences economic rent from the liability to fund the benefits that created that stream of value in the first place.

There are issues of concern with large-scale estimates of behaviour. Mason Gaffney identifies some of these:

- omitting all but numerical, monetary forms of wealth and income and social cost
- seeking to monetize the gains from synergy, and loss of synergy
- grasping the effects of symbiosis, as between a city and its rural hinterland
- fathoming the extensive implications of non-point pollution
- weighing the effects of patriotism, fellowship, spiritual values, family values
- acknowledging that, in natural habitats, some things should not be monetized
- remembering the value of the caring roles – mothers in the family, caring for aged members of the community

Unless handled honestly, the quest for hard numbers caters to the worst caricatures and travesties of what economics is about.

---

in relation to the way gross domestic product (GDP) misrepresents reality. That number is regularly mentioned in the media as if it is an authoritative guide to trends in the economy. It is seriously defective, but no government has had the courage to abandon its use. In offering a critique of official statistics, it is incumbent on us to offer alternatives while acknowledging the limits of our numbers.

The real-time measure of deadweight losses from taxation can be computed with greater accuracy in Australia and the United States than in the UK. Unlike the UK, those two countries compile statistics on land value for fiscal purposes. In the US, the tax authorities (federal and local) are legally obliged to distinguish the sources of "commercial rents".

▶ In most US states, tax assessors are required by law to report separately on land and building values.

▶ For federal income taxes (personal and corporate) landlords are required to estimate land values: they may depreciate buildings, but they may not tax-depreciate land.

The estimation of deadweight losses is hazardous when statistical agencies jumble economic rents with earned incomes. This cannot be used as an excuse for not attempting to quantify the impact of taxes, however. Scientists have worked out how to overcome the gravitational pull of Earth to send astronauts to the moon. It is not beyond their capacity to work out how the gravitational pull of the land beneath our feet, when aligned with malevolent taxes, prevents society from elevating itself onto a new trajectory of social evolution. The financial algorithms that facilitate this process are employed by the Danish Government to re-value land every two years.

The cross-checks

The gains achieved by reforming taxation are huge. This claim can be cross-checked with economies that do, indeed, draw a significant part of revenue directly from rent. The historian's method of counter-factual reasoning helps us to identify and quantify the divergent economic performances of culturally similar populations.

Chairman Mao versus Sun Yat-sen

If Chairman Mao had allowed mainland China to emulate the gravitational effects of the AGR model, which were at work among the Chinese of Hong Kong and Taiwan, how much richer would the republic of China be today?

Hong Kong enjoyed a head start under British colonial rule (see p.24 above). That is why she enjoys the highest per capita income (Table 5:1). Taiwan is hot on her heels. Communist China languishes far behind: her dismal record is based on 30 years of hybrid economics, trying to compress communism and capitalism into a single economic model. The difference in income cannot be explained in terms of differences in psychology, physiological or culture. The difference is in the economic models, the foundation element being the approach to public finance.

Statisticians can now estimate the losses that accrued in China over the 60 years since Taiwan introduced its land-and-tax reforms. Losses attributable

Table 5:1 **Economic outcomes in three Sino Societies** (selected indicators: 2015 estimates)			
	Taiwan	**Hong Kong**	**China**
GDP *per capita* (PPP): US$	46,800	56,700	14,100
Unemployment rate: %	3.8	2.9	4.2
Population below poverty: % (2012 estimates)	1.5	19.2	6.1
Source: CIA World Factbook: https://www.cia.gov/library/publications/the-world-factbook/geos/sf.html			

to the centrally planned economy amount to tens of trillions of dollars. But we cannot expect precision in the attempt to measure what could have been achieved if Sun Yat-sen's fiscal policies had prevailed when the Republic of China came into existence in 1911. Try to imagine how the quality of life would have been enhanced if China's productive potential had not been repressed by the ideologically-driven civil war in the decades before World War 2.

Statistics are important for testing theories, but they are not a substitute for clarity of thought. Consider, for example, the poverty rate recorded in Hong Kong. Defenders of the Treadmill Tax paradigm might argue that this level of poverty implied limits to what can be expected from the AGR model. The explanation, however, is this: *Hong Kong is a victim of its success.*

▶ During the communist era, the British colony attracted mainland refugees fleeing the Maoist regime. The gravitational pull of the colony's economic prosperity overwhelmed the repulsive power of the Bamboo Curtain!

▶ Following Brexit (Britain's lease ran out in 1997), the flow of economic migrants increased as people went in search of a better life. They compounded the demographic crisis on the rocky outcrop that is Hong Kong.

Despite the demographic pressures, however, the AGR model enabled Hong Kong to fund world-class infrastructure (such as the metro) and public housing limited by the geological constraints of a confined space.

Turning a curse into a virtue

We move to Africa for our second example, and switch from emphasis on surface rents to the resource rents that Joseph Stiglitz spotlighted in a recent book.

'A basic principle of economics holds that it is highly efficient to tax rents because such taxes don't cause any distortions. A tax on land rents doesn't make the land go away. Indeed, the great 19th century progressive Henry George argued that government should rely solely on such a tax. Today, of course, we realize that rents can take many forms – they can be collected not just on land, but on the value of natural resources like oil, gas, minerals, and coal. There are other sources of rents, such as those derived from the exercise of monopoly power. A stiff tax on all such rents would not only reduce inequality but also reduce incentives to engage in the kind of rent-seeking activities that distort our economy and our democracy.'[4]

Botswana is land-locked by the five countries listed in Table 5:2. She out-performs her neighbours as measured by GDP *per capita*. This cannot be explained in terms of differences in indigenous culture – they all shared a history going back to the Bantu migrations of 500 AD. The exceptional case is South Africa. The scale of European settlement and investment in that territory over the past century ought to have given the post-apartheid country a huge

---

4 Joseph Stiglitz (2012), *The Price of Inequality*, London: Allen Lane, pp.212-213. Emphasis added.

	Resource endowments	GDP *per capita* 2015 estimates: US $ (purchasing power parity)
Botswana	Diamonds, copper, nickel	16,400
Zimbabwe	Cotton, tobacco, gold	2,100
Angola	Oil, diamonds, gas	7,300
Namibia	Diamonds, copper, gold	11,400
Zambia	Copper, cobalt, electricity	3,900
South Africa	Diamonds, gold, platinum	13,200

Table 5:2 **Resource rich countries in Southern Africa**

Source: CIA World Factbook

economic advantage. The ANC government failed to capitalise on its natural resource endowments, however, and it terminated the local site-value tax in 2004.

The other four countries are classic post-colonial countries. In Zimbabwe, the failure to develop was a self-inflicted wound. The Mugabe government embarked on a destructive "land reform" programme that enriched the President's buddies but destroyed productivity. The other three countries were afflicted by what is called the "resource curse": rents of natural resources are extracted by mining corporations and repatriated to tax havens.

What happened in Botswana? When the British granted independence in 1966, Botswana was the third poorest country in the world, with a per capita GDP of about $70. She had 22 university graduates, 12 kilometres of tarmacked road in a vast territory, and no access to the sea. Between 1966 and 1980 she achieved the fastest rate of economic growth *in the world* (averaging an annual growth rate of 9%). The basis of this "miracle" is explained in *The Silver Bullet*. When diamonds were discovered, De Beers was invited to extract the precious stones. Aided by shrewd advice from a western lawyer, the deal was done on Botswana's terms. Diamond rents were invested in Botswana's social infrastructure. The country took off. Diamonds were not a curse: they became the nation's best friend.[5] What might have happened to incomes in the neighbouring countries if they had contractually bound their foreign investors on terms that ensured the resource rents were recycled back into the welfare of their countries?

---

5 Fred Harrison (2008), *The Silver Bullet*, London: theIU, p.51.

Bogus budgets

Statistics embedded by national treasuries in their budget statements are treated with reverence. No attempt is made to test the plans for changes to tax rates with estimates of deadweight losses. That would not be surprising in an authoritarian regime. But in the UK, the Bills that are submitted to Parliament for approval are offered with what purport to be assessments of the impact of the proposed changes to the law. And yet, the impact assessments omit data of the kind which would reveal that second- and third-best strategies were being enacted into law. Instead, sweeping assertions are offered which are calculated to deceive. This is illustrated by the opening two sentences in what turned out to be George Osborne's last Spending Review and Autumn Statement, presented to the House of Commons on 25 November, 2015.

> ' The first duty of government is to protect economic and national security, thereby allowing the government to extend opportunity for working people at every stage of their lives. The Spending Review and Autumn Statement delivers on that priority.' [6]

Validation of that claim was offered in terms of the increase in the number of people in employment. The chancellor was silent on the fact that most of those jobs were based on zero-hours contracts; the employment security of the UK's working population was deteriorating by the day, but that was not revealed in the official statistics.

To bolster the appearance that HM Treasury is guided by the principles of open and honest dealing, an Office for Budget Responsibility was established in 2011. The OBR was charged with scrutinising the Treasury's numbers, to provide an independent assessment for Parliament. And yet, in the documentation published by the OBR, there is no hint that fiscal policies themselves are seriously and routinely dislocating the economy. Can the OBR be accused of dereliction of duty? Its terms of reference are summarised on its website:

> ' The Budget Responsibility and National Audit Act sets out the overarching duty of the OBR to examine and report on the sustainability of the public finances. It also gives complete discretion to the OBR in the performance of its duties, as long as those duties are performed objectively, transparently and independently and takes into account the sitting government's policies *and not alternative policies*.' [7]

The emphasis is added. The Cameron government ensured that the OBR would test the Treasury's policies within the confines of conventional wisdom. The OBR was not free to suggest more effective policies for achieving the government's declared goals. But does that limitation on its terms of reference mean that the OBR is beyond criticism? It does not. *The OBR cannot provide a comprehensive assessment of taxes employed by the Treasury without calculating the deadweight losses.* If the government's tax tools undermine its

6 George Osborne (2015), *Spending Review and Autumn Statement*, Cm 9162, HM Treasury, November, p.1
7 http://budgetresponsibility.org.uk/topics/legislation-and-related-material/

declared aims and objects, that is information relevant to the proceedings in Parliament. Without that information, how can Parliament itself adhere to the democratic norms of transparency and accountability?

The OBR cannot fall back on the claim that there is a paucity of information. If that was the cause of its failure to provide a full audit of Treasury policies, it is under an obligation to report that problem to Parliament.

> Modern economies do employ the 'land tax' –
> Australia, to cite just one example – so the issue is
> not a question of faith but of political will.

The absence of vital information does account, in part, for the "democratic deficit". People cannot insist on plugging the financial deficit if they have no idea of the scale of the losses inflicted on them by government. If the deficit is not plugged, it will not be possible for Mrs May's government to achieve its goals. Everyone loses. And so, an obligation falls on all parties – government, Parliament and the people – to agree on the need for a numerical assessment of the deadweight losses imposed on Britain. Then, an informed electorate can affirm its mandate for change. The compelling reason for reform was attested by *The Economist* in these terms:

' Until a modern economy takes the plunge and introduces a land tax – and keeps it – it is hard to know if performance will match promise. "It is a question of faith" admits Stuart Adam, of the Institute for Fiscal Studies, a think-tank which backs the idea. Yet until its benefits are convincingly displayed, few politicians will feel like risking the wrath of the landowning lobby. In short, precious little has changed since [Henry] George was alive.' [8]

The empirical evidence is already to hand: modern economies do employ the "land tax" – Australia, to cite just one example – so the issue is not a question of faith but of political will.

Biting the bullet

An authentic democracy is defined by the willingness of the guardians of the public's welfare to accept responsibility for their actions. The reciprocal responsibility falls on the electorate, which is obliged to remain vigilant. Neither of these obligations can be sensibly met without the relevant information. To elevate the quality of decision-making in Westminster, reliable data is needed to guide decision-making.

---

8 *The Economist* (2015), "Why Henry George had a point", April 1.
http://www.economist.com/blogs/freeexchange/2015/04/land-value-tax

Today, public policy is guided by statistics that are not fit for purpose. HM Treasury and the Bank of England employ "targets" like the rate of inflation, and tools like the "neutral rate of interest". Given their record of failure, we can be forgiven for thinking that their statistics and targets are employed to make it appear as though the authorities know what they are doing. Deadweight losses tell us that they do not know what they are doing.

Without annual information on generated rents and deadweight losses, the performance of Parliament cannot be objectively assessed, and elected representatives cannot be held accountable.

To achieve a functionally fit form of governance, new statistics are required. To preside with wisdom over the laws of the land, Parliament needs regular re-assessments of the rents being generated in the UK. Net taxable income provides the best single numerical indicator of the health and wealth of communities at all levels – local, regional and national. HM Treasury and the statistical agencies have chosen not to compile data on economic rent. That omission needs to be corrected.

As part of the post-Brexit settlement, the people of Britain should assert their democratic right of access to two statistics.

▶ **Demand No. 1:** Parliament will publish an annual assessment of economic rent generated from all sources in the United Kingdom.

Economic productivity, and policies that affect communities and their natural habitats, are optimised when government collects revenue directly from economic rent. Joseph Stiglitz calls this "the 'Henry George' theorem", because "not only is the land tax non-distortionary, but also it is the 'single tax' required to finance the public good".[9]

▶ **Demand No. 2**: Parliament will command an assessment of the deadweight losses inflicted on the United Kingdom by Acts of Parliament.

Without this information, the performance of Parliament cannot be objectively assessed, and elected representatives cannot be held accountable. Parliament must enact a law which orders that, on an annual basis – when the Budget is submitted to the House of Commons for scrutiny – the Chancellor of the Exchequer will publish revised statistics on the rents generated within the UK over the previous 12 months; and on the increase or decrease in the

---

9 Anthony Atkinson and Joseph Stiglitz (1980), *Lectures on Public Economics*, London: McGraw-Hill, p.525.

deadweight losses arising from proposed changes to tax rates. Armed with that information, people may choose to mandate the reconstruction of their public finances.

For civil society, the choice is brutally clear. Either we bite the bullet and mandate the AGR reform, or we fall silent on problems like unemployment, poverty, inequality and the abuse we inflict on the natural world. If we shy away from restructuring our public finances, we have no choice but to retreat to a strategy of containment: of living as best we can, and without complaint, with the distortions and damage caused to people's lives by those of us who, having successfully "climbed on to the housing ladder", have become the legionnaires in defence of the culture of cheating.

The awkward question for Nicola Sturgeon

For Nicola Sturgeon, Brexit is another step towards independence. She ordered her troops to engage 2m people in a conversation about their wishes for Scotland. But they cannot reach informed judgements until the First Minister answers one awkward question: *why has her government failed to initiate the abolition of Income Tax?* By switching to annual ground rent, the Scottish economy would be enlarged by £12bn. This would begin to equalise economic power between Edinburgh and London. A new age of enlightenment and prosperity would be inaugurated.

The SNP's fear of losing tariff-free exports to the EU is baseless. Breaking with the UK would mean jumping from the frying pan into the fire. North Sea oil rents are drying up, and the prospects appear grim if the statistic that Ms Sturgeon appears to endorse – a £15 billion deficit in the budget (higher than Greece's as a percentage of GDP) – is to be believed.

- If a sovereign Scotland was invited to join the EU (far from certain), she would be relegated to the peripheral margins, joining Greece and Ireland.

- Scotland would lose the protection of the UK and become a hostage to the fortunes of Berlin and Paris, continuing to live on the edge, with much of her net income diverted from London to new centres of exploitation.

In response to Brexit, Ms Sturgeon announced a new growth commission. The answers are already known, so was this an exercise in kicking into the long grass the difficult political choices which the SNP now faces?

The commission's mandate: consider two issues.

First: how to reduce the deficit to a "sustainable level". Under the prevailing economic and fiscal paradigm, the deficit cannot be reduced by any means other than by reducing the quality of public services. The only way to simultaneously reduce government deficits and generate additional funds to expand public services is to rebalance the revenue system: cut taxes that distort the economy and raise revenue from ground rents.[1]

Second: which currency should Scotland prefer? Neither the euro, nor sterling – nor a Scottish sovereign currency – will address Scotland's problems. But blaming the euro for the EU's problems is false economics. Consider two common currency cases.

- **The dollar:** the 50 states if the USA suffer the same core/periphery problems as the EU, because its fiscal regime is as perverse as Europe's.

- **Sterling:** the 4 nations of the UK suffer the same core/periphery problems as the EU. Likewise, if Scotland created its own currency, that would not inoculate it against the lopsided outcomes endured in the USA or EU.

---

1 Roger Sandilands and Fred Harrison (2015), *Black Holes to Pots of Gold*, p.4. From http://www.slrg.scot/

The only way to create a balanced economy is to adopt the financial mechanism that prevents the centre from exploiting the outer regions.

Radical political action is needed. The SNP has the democratic mandate to change Scotland's destiny. The haemorrhage of brain and brawn from the western islands to Edinburgh, and from there on to London, is a historic process which operates to this day.[2] Rural populations are depleted, making it increasingly difficult to educate children marooned in their hamlets. This creates the demand for additional taxes to subsidise increasingly unviable settlements, which reinforces the implosive dynamic that continues until communities on the periphery die.

Meanwhile, sprawling metropolitan centres are also hollowed out. The SNP government's Community Empowerment Act (2016) provides funds to help rural settlements, but *Scotland needs a systemic solution which simultaneously revives rural and urban communities.* Responsibility for past failures must be shared by Westminster and Holyrood.

- **Westminster** champions taxes that discriminate against Scotland. Will the regressive VAT be abolished when UK has completed Brexit?

- **Holyrood:** misallocation of resources has discriminated against low-income families through, for example, education. Free university tuition is biased to favour middle-class students, while working-class children have seen their attainment standards decline, in part because of spending cuts.

Scotland should lead the campaign for a new political settlement in which the four nations reconfigure themselves

VAT & the New Vision

The UK government used VAT to collect £115.1 billion in 2015-16. VAT is regressive, and it imposes a deadweight loss of at least 100%. This means that it suppresses UK economic activity to the tune of at least £115,100,000,000 a year (the equivalent of the entire NHS budget). By replacing VAT with AGR, across the UK's four nations people would enjoy a new prosperity based on the doctrine that, if government "got off their backs", they would produce all the wealth and welfare they needed to enjoy contented lives.

in a federation of equals. But the gravitational pull of London would continue. The only way to equalise people's life chances across the political and economic space is through AGR reform. The net income could then be shared on an equitable basis.

With fiscal reform in place, the relationship with the EU could be resolved on mutually beneficial terms. Scottish exporters would be able to sell all their products within an enlarged UK economy even if Europe raised its tariff barrier.

The beauty of Brexit is that it gives the Scottish Government the privilege of acting as honest broker between the UK and EU: not by direct negotiation, but by leading by example. *Scotland has the power to drive change by becoming the champion of tax reform.* That reform is fully elaborated by the Scottish Land Revenue Group: http://www.slrg.scot/

2 http://blogserver.cne-siar.gov.uk/wp-cnesleader/?p=947

6

Untangling the perverse web

THERESA MAY was married in a church built with money made from slavery. Her father had been the Vicar of the Church of St Mary the Virgin in Wheatley, Oxfordshire. The church was built in 1857 by the Rev. Edmund Elton, whose family fortune was partly based on the West Indian slave trade.[1]

That slice of shameful British history flashed through the mind of the Rev. Paul Nicolson as he stood in front of magistrates, accused of refusing to pay the property tax on the church-owned house which he occupied. The retired vicar counted the Elton family among his ancestors. He was the son of a rich champagne merchant, and his ancestral history – and Theresa May's marriage – reminded him of the mortal realities of life in Britain in the 21st century. The outlawing of slavery had not redeemed a society in which a baby's life chances turned on the postcode where he or she was born.

Theresa May's predecessor, David Cameron, had launched the Conservative government's "life chances" agenda. Reforms to enhance the quality of people's lives included a revision of tax-funded benefits, and the ordination of a "national living wage". Paul Nicolson was not duped by the veneer of political rhetoric. Under the current tax regime, Mrs May would not be able to achieve her declared aim of uniting everyone through shared prosperity. She could not do so, because magistrates across the land enforced a fiscal regime that taxed the state benefits of low-income families. What the state giveth, the state taketh with the property tax and the "bedroom tax" (a charge that cuts welfare benefits when the state decides that low-income families occupy bedroom space in excess of their needs). These cruel injustices led Paul Nicolson to his act of civil disobedience, and the risk of serving time in one of Her Majesty's Prisons.

In a letter he wrote to *The Church Times*, the angry Anglican clergyman stressed that the human right to life was honoured in the breach for people who lost out in the postcode lottery:

---

1 Margaret Elton (1994), *Annals of the EtonFamily, Bristol Merchants & Somerset Landowners*, Stroud: Alan Sutton Publishing, p.225.

' I was born in Kensington in 1932 in the Courtfield ward, to the fourth generation of a family who had done well in the wine and spirit trade. My grandmother was an Elton. *According to the Office of National Statistics my life expectancy is 92 years.* I retired to Tottenham in 1999 where life expectancy in the next door ward of *Northumberland Park is 72 years.* I am embarrassed by the fact that people born in that ward in the same year as myself died fourteen years ago.'

The length of life one might reasonably expect to enjoy on earth is a key indicator of one's life chances. In the UK, for millions of people the human right to life is denied. In 2013 alone, more than 63,000 people under the age of 75 died needlessly. Given the availability of medical knowledge and technology, they ought to have lived longer lives. They died, and the reasons were analysed by Eurostat, the European Union's statistical agency.[2]

▶ UK performance was poorer than Slovenia's, the east European country whose resources fell far short of those at the disposal of the UK.

▶ The UK could derive no comfort from out-performing Slovakia, whose GDP (PPP) *per capita* was US$28,000, far short of the UK's $39,000.

To blame the appalling number of avoidable deaths on the UK's health service (the NHS) is unreasonable.[3] The health service is seriously under-funded. But why was the much poorer Slovenia able to outperform the fifth richest nation on the planet? Part of the answer is that the UK is constructed on the economics of apartheid. Millions of people live in poverty, and financial segregation is formalised in the spatial dispersal of the excluded. They are automatically displaced into ghettoes of poverty.

According to the late Dr George Miller, a distinguished epidemiologist, the tax-led maldistribution of income was directly responsible for the premature deaths of about 50,000 people in England and Wales alone. Every year, that number of people succumbs to the stresses of deprivation in all its complex forms, dying unnecessarily many years before their time should have been up.[4] How many years-of-life do they lose? In her study on *Why fight Poverty?* Julia Unwin – Chief Executive of the Joseph Rowntree Foundation – acknowledges a 7-year gap between those who live in the most deprived neighbourhoods compared to the UK average. The reality is more horrendous than that statistical comparison, and it haunts the waking hours of Paul Nicolson

For much of his working life, Nicolson ministered to his flock in a rustic part of the Home Counties. His idyllic village was the parish used as the location for the TV sitcom Vicar of Dibley. When he retired to Tottenham, in north London, he realised that he was living near a ward where people live, on average,

---

2 "The avoidable deaths in 2013" (2016), Brussels: Eurostat News Release, May 24. http://ec.europa.eu/eurostat/documents/2995521/7335847/3-24052016-AP-EN.pdf/4dd0a8ad-5950-4425-9364-197a492d3648
3 Charlie Haynes and Stephen Adams (2016), "NHS blamed as third of Britons die 'needlessly'", Daily Mail, June 5.
4 G.J. Miller (2003), Dying for Justice, London: Centre for Land Policy Studies, p.1.

17 fewer years than residents in one of the wards in the London borough of Kensington and Chelsea, where he was born.[5] He felt the injustice personally.

Outraged, he launched Taxpayers Against Poverty. His campaign led him to his act of civil disobedience. He refused to pay his Council Tax as a protest against the way impoverished families were being treated.[6] When David Cameron convened a conference in London to orchestrate action against corporations that seek fiscal refuge in tax havens, the reverend identified the wider issues in a letter to the chairmen of two parliamentary committees. He wrote:

' International and national wealthy and corrupt individuals not only launder their money through buying UK land, they also move the rents tax free into overseas banks.

Meanwhile the Treasury take steps to tax the incomes of UK citizens who cannot escape governmental clutches. Thoroughly to tackle the consequences of imported corruption, in the politically supported UK free market in land, the Prime Minister should also remove the profound injustice done to the landless tenants of the UK. According to the 2011 census 58.2% of households in Haringey rent their homes, 47% in London and 33% in England. Their shredded benefit incomes have been taxed by 250 councils since 2013 and diminished by ever increasing rents.

They are summoned in their tens of thousands for late and non-payment of council tax to the magistrates' courts. The magistrates then blindly pile the councils' enforcement costs in bulk on thousands of cases at a time in their absence [of which there are] around 3.5 million a year.

Those costs are blindly piled on top of the council tax arrears, other debts and against the already hungry, the disabled, those whose benefits have been stopped for three months with a sanction, in the processes of eviction, due to ever increasing rents, and with mental health problems, often followed by a visit from the bailiffs adding their fees; many who were not already hungry become so because of this onslaught on their inadequate incomes. All the government's protestations of care for vulnerable people bring to mind stable doors being shut after horses have bolted.[7]

Unlike The Experts who agonise over poverty, Paul Nicolson understood the need to supplement palliatives with structural reforms. People in urgent need of access to food banks should have their suffering alleviated. But government has the responsibility to shift policy in the direction of reforms that would abolish poverty.

Birthrights and wrongs

The causal links between taxes and premature death are not obvious, at first glance. That is testimony to the shrewd skills of generations of aristocrats in

5 Fred Harrison (2016), "The $14 trillion Lift-off from the Great Stagnation", in *Rent Unmasked* (ed: Fred Harrison), London: Shephard-Walwyn, p.133.
6 Roswynne Jones (2016), "Reverend Paul Nicolson: Retired Anglican vicar ready to go to jail in his battle for poor", *Daily Mirror*, July 31.
7 May 12, 2016 letter, posted on http://www.taxpayersagainstpoverty.org.uk/more-people-should-undertstand-why-there-is-hunger-in-the-uk-the-corrupt-buy-our-land-and-move-the-rents-overseas/

Parliament. Their *raison d'être* was the plunder of the public purse, a plunder that continues to this day. Understanding – and confronting head-on – that connection between fiscal history and its mortal effects is the pre-condition for plans to equalise people's life chances.

The tax regime transmits its malign influence through laws and institutions that ring-fence the privileges which degrade the people whose ancestors had been cast off the commons in favour of flocks of sheep. The social influence of that history continues to course through communities to this day, its lethal effects transmitted into people's lives, bearing down on the physical and mental wellbeing of those who are born as losers. The process of exclusion is enshrined by many customs and practises, not least the inability to acquire a home. Newspapers routinely expose the essence of this deprivation in all its forms, including one headline which announced: "The young poor are kept out of top careers by lack of family connections",[8] Less conspicuous is the psycho-biological impacts of these social processes.

Each person embodies the complex interaction between three forces: biological, psychological and sociological. Science has advanced to the point where we can describe the interaction of these three elements in fine detail. So, for example, dissonant social experiences affect our psychological health, which simultaneously affects our bodies. The transmission mechanisms include the release of the hormone cortisol as a result of stress, which diverts oxygen to the muscles, and can result in sleep deprivation and fatigue. Acute discomfort affects the immune system. The brain transmits signals of threats both real and imagined. If we are constantly bombarded by influences that drain us of our physical and mental energy, the prospects of a long and comfortable life are diminished.

The Welfare State was supposed to mitigate the impact of deprivation through the provision of health, education and social security. It succeeded for some, but failed the millions of people who continue to suffer the indignities inherited from the exclusion that began with the land-grabs of old. The Welfare State itself cannot be blamed for the shortfall in its performance. Post-war Labour governments knew that social reform had to be instituted in tandem with tax reform. As recently as 1931 the legislation that enacted the AGR model was guided through Parliament by a Labour chancellor (Philip Snowden). His Act could have been retrieved from the Westminster archives and reintroduced in 1945. Winston Churchill, who had championed that reform in 1909, was the war hero who still presided as leader of the Tory Party in opposition. It is reasonable to assume that he would have supported fiscal reform on terms that run with the grain of both market and moral sensibilities. Instead, Labour governments – which had been granted political mandates for change – made a strategic error. They wrapped their land and housing policies in socialist garb.

---

8 Rebecca English (2016), *Daily Mail*, July 27.

Failure was predictable.[9] Once again, the rent-seeking culture bequeathed by the late medieval aristocracy triumphed. Its legacies of deprivation manifest themselves in many forms.

▶ People classified as lower class are deprived of self-worth. "Know your place" is not a term now used in polite company, but it resonates with people who, in the US, are called "trailer trash".

▶ Low-value zones are not referred to as ghettoes, but they tell the world that the occupants are not capable of acquiring their own properties without the financial support of others.

▶ Absence of jobs that pay living wages inflict the indignity of being dependent on welfare benefits. Compensation is sought in "comfort" food and stimulants to dull the predicaments in life.

▶ Memory deprivation accompanies material deprivation. Contrast the families that live in 3-generation spans, with the aristocracy and their intergenerational memories spanning centuries, their ancestors etched in technicolour oil paintings hung on their palatial walls.

These are just a few of the routes by which deprivation selects and assaults its victims, in a social process that I have termed humanicide.[10] Language is another lethal mechanism, one that looms large in the discussion on education reform. If we fail to reshape the language of everyday discourse, the bid by Theresa May's government to equalise life chances by erasing the barriers to enhanced outcomes in education will again be defeated by the culture of rent-seeking.

The grammar of inequality

Theresa May shocked the political class by disclosing that she would restore the role of grammar schools in the education system. The reaction was overwhelmingly hostile. Her initiative was interpreted through the prism of the socialist critique of inequality which had prevailed since 1945. The discourse was distorted with loaded language, such as the "brightest and best" being "selected" for privileged treatment in grammar schools, with the "failures" from "poor backgrounds" once again disadvantaged. The post-war binary choice between children who qualified for a grammar education, and those who were sent to "secondary" schools, was a horrifying prospect. Unfortunately, Mrs May had presented her proposals by playing into the language that constrained the imagination of what was needed to liberate the needs of all children.

---

9 V.H. Blundell (1994), "Flawed Land Acts 1947-1976", in Nicolaus Tideman (ed.), *Land and Taxation*, London: Shepheard Walwyn.
10 Fred Harrison (2012), *The Traumatised Society*, London: Shepheard-Walwyn, Ch.4.

Mrs May's goal was to move in the direction of assessing the needs of every child, to cater for individual needs and abilities. She wanted to correct the unfairness that remained embedded in the system. She was aware of the harsh economic realities that had thwarted attempts to equalise educational opportunities through the comprehensive schools that were created in large part by Margaret Thatcher.

▶ Selection continued to discriminate through the ability of high-income families to buy houses in the catchment areas of high-achieving schools.

The locational attributes of a good education is a lesson in the sponge effect of the land market. The owners of properties near high-performance state schools could put a price on the net gains to be reaped by a good education. In 2016, the price they extracted averaged £53,000.[11]

▶ Private schools receive tax relief amounting to about £700m a year. That helps to keep down the cost of school fees for families that could afford private education.

The subsidised fees put private education within the reach of a larger number of families. The net gains are capitalised into higher house prices for properties near the private day schools. No child born in Britain can escape this fiscal-driven inheritance. State and private education systems are underpinned by the choices made by government on how the nation's net income is distributed, used and abused.

It is possible, of course, to point to many successes – people like Mrs May, daughter of a clergyman who was educated in a grammar school girl who went on to become Prime Minister. And some boys from secondary modern schools turned themselves into millionaire entrepreneurs. But the fact that some individuals can escape their circumstances does not illustrate how grammar schools, *per se*, overcome the underlying financial injustice.

The objection to grammar schools is an oblique critique of systemic discrimination, as illustrated by the use of the notion of social mobility. The objective is said to be one of empowering children to move from the "lower class" to a higher class. But talking in those terms reinforces a social model which presupposes that, if children from low-income families are to move upwards, children near the top must move downwards. There is no win-win outcome: one winner must mean one loser. That prospect is anathema to the home-owning middle class. And so they support the campaign to preserve non-selective comprehensive schools even while many of them deploy their purchasing power to give their offspring private tuition and a home near high-achieving schools. To reinforce the educational advantages, their children are provided with social

11 Christopher Hope and Steven Swinford (2016), "Stop school selection by house price, says May" *Daily Telegraph*, 9 September.

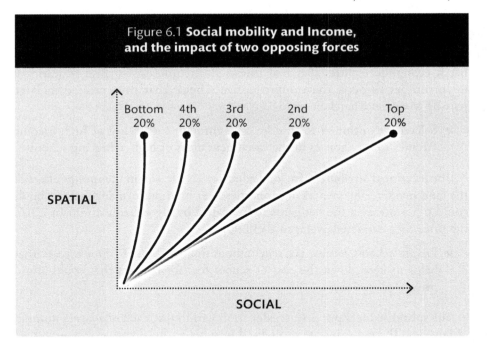

Figure 6.1 **Social mobility and Income, and the impact of two opposing forces**

contacts and are imbued with attitudes and expectations which steer them towards the Good Life on grounds other than merit. Opposition to educational selection becomes a way to preserve the rent-seeking culture!

The freedom to improve one's life chances rests on a mobility that is two-dimensional: social and spatial. Progress depends on the willingness to study at school and, subsequently, deliver value-for-money in work. But mobility is also contingent on spatial imperatives, which under the current arrangements repress personal fulfilment. No matter how good the school, if the gravitational forces from the spatial dimension are repressive, a child finds it difficult to elevate out of the status into which he or she was born. This is schematically illustrated in Figure 6:1.

Children in families located in the upper class tiers, composed of the top 20% of income-and-asset brackets, are not constrained by spatial barriers. Their parents own high-value homes, and they are imbued with the personal characteristics that rate highly with prospective employers. Going down this scale, children find themselves increasingly constrained by non-academic forces. All the characteristics that define poverty, which are carefully chronicled and associated with locations like parts of Tottenham in London and Blackpool in the north-west of England, militate against a child's prospects. If it's not house prices (which drive low-income workers out of London), or not the low income of parents, then it's the general character of the economy: prospects are rationed by (ultimately) the tax regime that crushes creativity out of the population at large.

Since the time of Margaret Thatcher, the pressures from the spatial component of mobility have reinforced social immobility. Thatcher initiated the privatisation of social housing, which expanded the number of families sitting on capital gains (by swallowing resources out of the public purse). But this did not enhance the quality of people's lives, in general, or expand the prospects of future generations. Over a sustained period of 13 years, the median household suffered a fall in real incomes after deducting for housing costs. And there will be a further constraint on social mobility with the decline in the proportion of families that own their homes.

The OECD joined the attack on Theresa May. Its education expert, Andreas Schleicher, impoverished the debate by persisting with the language of "meritocracy", which draws attention to "the brightest students" who are selected for a tailored education, conveying the implicit message that non-bright children must be dim. To compound the unhelpful nature of his intervention, he offered as his clinching argument against the UK education system the evidence gathered by the OECD which ranked Singapore and Hong Kong at the top of the educational achievement league.[12] What was special about Singapore and Hong Kong? Schleicher failed to connect education with the social *milieu*, which is framed by fiscal governance that maximises the incentives for personal achievement.

In Britain, low-income families do not seek to diminish the prospects for children of high-income families. All they want is a square deal, in which *unearned privileges* do not serve as barriers to their lives. Equalising life chances does not mean diminishing anyone's *earned rewards*. But managing the affairs of the poor by numbers (such as reserving a certain number of spaces in schools for the "disadvantaged") is demeaning. It does not undermine the rent-seeking culture, and it cannot provide a template for the emancipation of every child born in Britain. The language of "meritocracy" perpetuates the economics of apartheid, consolidating the class-based boundaries that segregate people into winners and losers.

The philosophical abyss

Shortcomings in the education system are one of the institutional symptoms of a pathologically perverse tax regime. For generations, politicians have twisted their doctrines every which way without finding a route out of the cycles of deprivation. Whenever there is an apparent breakthrough, the next property boom/bust intervenes to reverse the gains and deepen the divide between rich and poor. The transmission mechanism is no longer the voting power of the aristocracy. The political baton has been passed to middle-class home owners.

---

12 Helen Warrell (2016), "OECD criticises proposal to bring back grammar schools", *Financial Times*, Sept. 16.

Box 6:1 **Home-owners and the Rent-Seekers' Charter**

According to the Taxpayers' Alliance (TPA), the average household in the top 20% of income earners will pay £1,686,970 in tax over the working lifetime. The calculation is based on Office for National Statistics data for 2016. TPA wants government to reduce the tax burden by being more efficient in the way it spends the public's taxes. It does not note that the top 20% of income recipients are also the biggest winners from the State's handout of welfare benefits.[1]

According to the estate agency Rightmove, terraced properties in London's Kensington had an average sold price of £4,507,685 and semi-detached properties averaged £7,633,846 in the 12 months to August 2016. What does that mean for the owner of a (say) £5m residential property, who would be in the top 20% bracket? With house prices rising at conservatively estimated rates of increase between 2017 and 2021 (with a weakening of prices in 2019), that owner will have pocketed an increase in tax-funded windfall capital gains of £1,700,000. The home owner will have been reimbursed for his whole lifetime tax liabilities in five years flat. Assuming the 18-year property cycle continues through to 2026, which marks the end of the current house price cycle, that property will have more than doubled in value to over £12m.

- Capital gains are the measure of the value of public services which the owners of residential property enjoy free-of-charge under the Rent-seeker's Charter. Their subsidies are not means-tested.

- Those public services are funded, in part, by low-income taxpayers who live in rented accommodation. Their taxes are not refunded through housing-related windfalls.

This State-sponsored device for making the rich richer (and the poor, poorer) means that, for most of their lives, rich folk enjoy public services without paying for them.[2]

1 http://www.taxpayersalliance.com/lifetime_tax_2016
2 Harrison (2006), *Ricardo's Law*, Ch.1.

They accumulate land-based capital gains under the illusion that these are earned over a working lifetime. The New Aristocracy is the high-end home-owner who enjoys a tax-free life, riding on the backs of tenants who pay rents to landlords and taxes to the government (see Box 6:1).

But pessimism is not warranted. Our world has entered what Joseph P. Overton (1960–2003), an American public policy analyst, called a window of opportunity. He contended that popular opinion determines which policies were within the realm of political acceptability. If a policy did not fall within that window, politicians seeking office would not entertain it, irrespective of their personal preferences. Figure 6:2 illustrates the Overton thesis in terms of the rise and fall of the politics of slavery, the institution that made some of Paul Nicolson's ancestors rich.

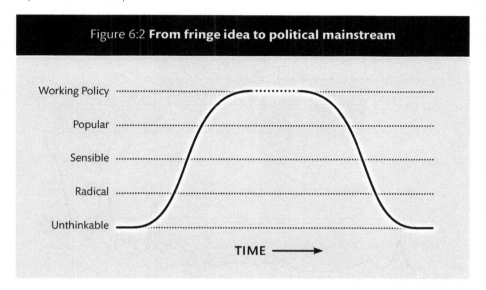

Figure 6:2 **From fringe idea to political mainstream**

Once upon a time, it was unthinkable for society to legitimise slavery. Then, as commercial opportunity emerged, slavery rose up the scale of public comprehension to become an acceptable way of making money. Bristol merchants were enriched by transporting slaves across the Atlantic. The Yorkshire mills consumed the cotton supplied by the slave plantations of America. Slavery was enshrined as a working policy of the British Empire; until, one day, thanks to the inflamed moral sensibilities of a small group of people, this way of treating humans began to lose its acceptability. Finally, the policy-makers determined that slavery was unconscionable. At that point, as it became unthinkable, it was outlawed.

The AGR model was acceptable to the peoples of the population for 50 years (from the 1890s to the 1930s); so much so, that it was twice enshrined in law. But the nobility retained its influence over Parliament. The law was not implemented. Over the following 50 years the AGR model of public finance fell outside the realm of acceptability. Today, however, public perceptions have shifted in the direction of change. The immediate future is one of creativity and progress; or, the political void will be filled by dark forces.

In prescribing a reform of governance based on the AGR model, we are not groping in a vacuum. Some politicians are alert to the possibilities of reshaping their mandates. One of them is Dr Vince Cable. He served as Business Secretary in David Cameron's coalition government (2010-2015), tackling the fall-out from the 2008 crisis. In his inquest on those events he acknowledged that the dysfunctional housing market exercised "powerful negative consequences". Many countries were victims of the cycles that disrupt the economy. Could this repetitiveness provide the incentive for fiscal reform?

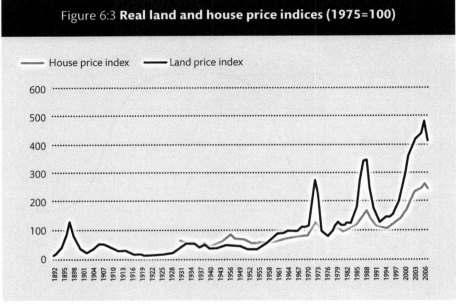

Figure 6:3 **Real land and house price indices (1975=100)**

Note: House and land data for war years are interpolated.
Source: Paul Cheshire. http://blogs.lse.ac.uk/politicsandpolicy/land-prices-the-dog-thats-lost-its-bark/

'In the UK, arguably, property, and particularly domestic property, performs a similar role. Fred Harrison has argued that there is a long-term property cycle of around seventeen [sic] years which is highly correlated with the wider economic cycle. In an upswing, confidence grows, encouraging consumption, and there is an associated boom in home improvements, while increased building spills over into construction products and furnishings. Certainly, the three booms and busts experienced by my generation – in 1974/5, 2002/2 and 2008/9 – fit that pattern.' [13]

The predictability of the trends can be displayed on a graph (Figure 6:3). The rise and fall of land values is repetitive. My attempts to alert Tony Blair to this pattern of history in 1997, when he arrived in Downing Street, fell on deaf ears. His chancellor, Gordon Brown, while cynically exploiting the language of change ("no more booms and busts"), confined his actions to measures that would permit the land price cycle to flourish all the way to the peak in prices in the third quarter of 2007. Northern Rock, a mortgage bank, was the first victim. On 14 September the bank sought salvation – a cash injection – from the Bank of England. Britain endured a devastating economic crisis. This episode was avoidable in theory, but not in terms of practical politics.

Tony Blair's fate is a warning to Theresa May. He had adequate time to anticipate the crisis of 2008. A full 10 years before prices peaked in 2007, I wrote not only to Blair, but communicated with letters to four of his inner

---

13 Vince Cable (2015), *After the Storm*, London: Atlantic Books, p.243.

Box 6:2 **Passing the buck for 2008**

Alastair Campbell was Tony Blair's No. 10 spin doctor. My letter to him recalled the 1997 letter which I had addressed to him, which warned of the 2007 house price peak. Because of the failure to reform the tax regime, I asserted that the government's policies were a "shambles". His reply, dated February 5, 2003, stated:

> ' I'm a little bemused as to why you believe this country's economic policy is "a shambles". These are difficult times for the global economy but pretty well every independent expert believes this country is in better shape to weather these storms than our competitors. That's surely in large part a result of the economic policies followed by this government.'

When Britain's financial sector went into freefall in 2008, the Labour government – now led by Blair's Chancellor of the Exchequer, Gordon Brown – blamed the crisis on the global financial system.

circle of ministers and advisers in Downing Street. The warning was stark and simple: they had a decade in which to revamp the fiscal system. I explained that, without reform, a depression would follow the bust. The prognosis was recorded in a book published in 1997.[14] It was based solely on the repetitive cycles in the land market, the dynamics of which I had documented in *The Power in the Land*. But either the comprehension or the political will was absent. When I followed up with a warning letter in 2003, Blair's Press Officer in Downing Street would have none of it (see Box 6:2).

Blair was consumed by the hubris of power, and he chose to disregard my warnings.[15] The biggest price was paid by people who traditionally vote for Blair's Labour Party. But it would be fair to add that politicians like Blair are ill-served by the civil servants in Whitehall. They fail to support the policy-makers with the information needed to deliver enlightened governance.

Given the harshness of the fall-out from 2008, can we expect politicians like Vince Cable, who are now consulted as public commentators, to guide the discourse in a new direction for the next generation of politicians? Will the UK enjoy leadership based on integrity and be empowered to untangle the perverse web of deceit? Or will the tax regime continue to asphyxiate the British economy?

---

14 Fred Harrison (1997), *The Chaos Makers*, London: Vindex.
15 Fred Harrison (2005), *Boom Bust: House Prices, Banking and The Depression of 2010* (2005), London: Shepheard-Walwyn; *2010 The Inquest* (2010), available at http://www.sharetherents.org/wp-content/uploads/2013/09/2010-The-Inquest-FINAL.pdf and reported in http://www.moneymorning.com.au/20160415/how-to-profit-from-news-in-the-economy-before-its-even-written.html and http://www.theepochtimes.com/n3/2000510-economists-explain-why-our-economy-crashes-every-18-years/?photo=6

The art of wrecking habitats

Institutionalised corruption — the kind which corrodes culture and communities — is on publicly display in the customs and practices employed by the European Union. Rural settlements, and natural habitats, are among the victims. These outcomes are not intentional. But they illustrate the terrible price that is paid when law-makers and their enforcers fail to interrogate the nature of the power they exercise. Vandalism is necessarily perpetrated when taxes are levied on people's earned incomes, and when subsidies are distributed without understanding the impacts which they sanction under the laws of the land.

Without food, a population cannot sustain itself. Food security is paramount, but can the EU justify devoting 40% of its budget to "agriculture"? Farmers generate a tiny fraction of the value produced in Europe (see table). Are anti-social influences at work which have nothing to do with food security?

The Common Agricultural Policy distributes £42 billion extracted from the pay packets of European employees. Almost £3bn is received by UK beneficiaries. As much as 80% of those subsidies to the agricultural sector are reaped by 25% of those engaged in farming. The payments are not made for the purpose of growing food.

Guardian columnist George Monbiot expressed outrage that "Russian oligarchs, Saudi princes and Wall Street bankers have bought up tracts of European farmland, thus qualifying for the vast sums we shovel into their pockets. The shareholders of Tate & Lyle, the sugar corporation, have enjoyed this sweetener, picking up a total of €764m. Why is no word raised against these benefit tourists?"[1]

The CAP enriches the owners of land, while leaving the majority of producers - their tenant - living on the breadline. Working farmers are vulnerable to the most insidious disease afflicting rural communities: suicide. Scottish farmer Dr Duncan Pickard has concluded that agriculture needs a financial revolution: subsidies should be scrapped and replaced with the AGR policy. This, he explains, is the only way to prevent subsidies inflating land prices and excluding young people from getting a foothold in the farm sector. He concludes that "The high price of land makes it impossible for newcomers who are not already rich, to start farming. *More food could be produced in the UK, but is not, because subsidies allow farmers to use their land below its optimal potential.* I define subsidies as non-means-tested income support for wealthy landowners".[2]

1 http://www.monbiot.com/2016/06/21/leave-well-alone/
2 Duncan Pickard (2016), "Enlightenment's Food for Thought", in *Rent Unmasked* (ed: Fred Harrison), London: Shepheard-Walwyn, p.205.

GDP Sectoral Composition (2015): % Selected EU Countries			
	AGRI-CULTURE	INDUSTRY	SERVICES
UK	0.6	19.7	79.6
Germany	0.7	30.2	69.1
Spain	2.5	22.7	74.8
Greece	3.9	13.3	82.8
Ireland	1.5	24.9	73.5

To sustain the claim that the EU sponsors institutionalised corruption, we have to show that this is a necessary outcome of its financial procedures. That evidence was gathered by an accountant who was hired to reshape the EU's accounting techniques. Marta Andreasen established that the EU was "an open till waiting to be robbed". But when she insisted on tightening the rules, she was fired. Spain provides one example of financial malpractice. It involved the cultivation of high-grade flax. The subsidies were worth five times the support available for cereals, so farmers responded to the price signal: they raised cultivation from 186 hectares to 91,000 hectares. But the flax was of such low-grade that there was no market for it. Much of the crop for which grants were claimed was fictitious.[3]

But the greatest damage is not of the law-breaking sort. It is the kind that covertly distorts the way people go about their business, as illustrated by the EU's "structural funds". These subsidies are supposed to reduce rural poverty. Instead, they wreck communities.

- **EU-funded highways** boost land prices in marginal areas, driving house prices beyond the means of local people; in turn, causing
- **the exodus of young people** with skills: the quest for jobs in the core cities deplete rural communities; while the
- **taxable income (rents)** are sucked out of villages and into big towns, rendering life harder for low-income families in Madrid, Paris and Rome; so
- **provoking politicians** into trying to ride out-of-control property booms with regressive taxes (VAT) and austerity-driven "reforms".

Accompanying the wrecking of human settlements is the damage to the habitats created and sustained by nature. The owners of marginal uplands are subsidised to use their land for sheep rearing, in the process clearing the wildlife from their habitats in forests and streams. This subjects downstream urban settlements to periodic flooding. The misuse of the uplands, for the purpose of squeezing rents out of the public purse, deprives land of its capacity to absorb rainwater. Result: heavy rainfalls are not contained in the upland fields; instead, gushing down rivers and into people's homes.

Ecologist Peter Smith, who runs two nature reserves in England, estimates that in the UK between 40% and 50% of the land could be shared with wildlife to the mutual benefit of both nature and society.[4] But to achieve benign outcomes, he argues, a rental price has to be put on nature. Some conservationists find that proposition anathema, but Smith explains that the problem is not with putting a value on nature but with not valuing nature properly. The rent-based fiscal ethos would equip society to live in harmony with nature, and empower conservationists to save endangered species.

---

3 Marta Andreasen (2009), *Brussels Laid Bare*, Yelverton: St Edwards Press, p.13.

4 Peter Smith (2016), "Cries of the Wild", in *Rent Unmasked*, p.243.

7

The mandate

I MAGINE the scene. The gynaecological ward of a hospital in Stockton-on-Tees, a town in the north-eastern corner of England. A mother lies in bed, her first-born son cuddled into her chest. The father stands proud, a big smile creasing his face. The gynaecologist who delivered the baby enters to assure them that their baby was healthy: his vital signs were good, and they could take him home. That prognosis was not the truth, the whole truth, and nothing but the truth. The doctor knew that the odds were stacked against the boy: he was about to embark on a lifetime's voyage whose terminal end could be forecasted with reasonable accuracy.

The medical notes disclosed the parent's address. From this, the doctor was able to infer the baby's life chances. The doctor could not bring himself to utter the words, but his conscience prevents him from leaving the parents in ignorance. He places a sheet of paper on the bedside table and exits the ward.

The father, puzzled, picks up the document. It is published by Public Health England and the text is headed *Stockton-on-Tees Health Profile 2015*. The date: June 2, and the second paragraph reveals the heart-breaking news. The father chokes as he reads the words to his wife:

' Life expectancy is 17.3 years lower for men and 11.4 years lower for women in the most deprived areas of Stockton-on-Tees than in the least deprived areas.'

The parents were born and raised – and then married – in one of those deprived areas in the town which, two centuries ago, gave birth to the railway revolution. The child's life was prejudiced before he was discharged from hospital. No legal argument about his human rights in the Royal Court of Justice in London would change the odds: they favoured the death of the boy 17 years before boys born on the same day, in the same hospital, whose families lived in prosperous areas. Britain's "unwritten constitution" would not come to the rescue of that child, whose premature death is sealed by Acts of Parliament.

The fatal void between fine words and cruel practice is not peculiar to Britain. It is common to all western democracies. Nor is it a puzzle. Long ago, philosopher John Locke provided a neat definition of natural rights. He summarised these as everyone's right to "life, liberty and estate [land]". Take away one of those rights and a person is not, by definition, free to live a full life. In our world, a person may seek redress against anyone who threatens to curtail his life, or who attempts to deprive him of liberty through unlawful imprisonment. No such enforcement exists on the right to land. The "rule of law" mocks those who cannot muster the funds to buy a slice of the kingdom.

Brexit could be the opportunity to change this and leave its mark on the British constitution, through a Bill of Rights that enshrines a new doctrine of rights.

Brexit has also created a constitutional opportunity for the European Union. The mandate for revisions to the European Convention needs to be based on a pan-European conversation about the relationship of the individual to the State, and of the terms of the relationship between member States. One starting point for that conversation is the event that took place on December 10, 1948. The General Assembly of the United Nations proclaimed the Universal Declaration of Human Rights. The two clauses of Article 25 spelt out the right to an adequate standard of living, granting the individual the legal right to enforce that quality of life against governments that subverted it.

1. Everyone has the right to a standard of living adequate for the health and well-being of himself and of his family, including food, clothing, housing and medical care and necessary social services, and the right to security in the event of unemployment, sickness, disability, widowhood, old age or other lack of livelihood in circumstances beyond his control.

2. Motherhood and childhood are entitled to special care and assistance. All children, whether born in or out of wedlock, shall enjoy the same social protection.

But as we have seen, children do not "enjoy the same social protection".

The spirit of Article 25 was enshrined by the architects of the new Europe in their Convention for the Protection of Human Rights and Fundamental Freedoms. That document was drafted in 1950 by the Council of Europe and it came into force on 3 September 1953. Europe's Welfare States sought to honour these rights. None did more to equalise people's life chances than the United Kingdom. And yet, as Theresa May pointedly observed when she sought the job of Prime Minister: *children born into poverty die, on average, nine years earlier than those born into prosperous families.*

Mrs May's statistic is bad enough. But the average loss of life is 17 years for babies born in some areas of Glasgow and London, compared to the lives enjoyed by babies born on the same day in areas like Kensington and Chelsea. This renders bizarre the notion of human rights. In preparing a new Bill of Rights for Britain, therefore, the first task is for people to understand how they are deprived of their human rights, so that they may mandate the practical remedies in the new Bill of Rights.

Rights and responsibilities

The human rights doctrine is based on a caricature of the individual. This spawned two fatal deficiencies in the way the doctrine of human rights was applied.

1. People are conceived as private, isolated individuals. For practical purposes the social component of their personalities is ignored.

Humans are fusions of two layers of reality. The private characteristics enable each person to stand out from the crowd. Overwhelmingly, however, humans are composites of social characteristics. People become fully formed personalities when they absorb their share of the social assets of their community. Those assets include language, moral codes and the knowledge accumulated by previous generations. They also include the right to participate in the activities which produce the resources that made those social attributes possible, and which can only be sustained on a social basis.

2. Missing from the ascription of a personal "human right" – such as the right to work, or housing – was the means to enforce that right against others.

The son of a low-income family from the back streets of Stockton-on-Tees cannot assert his right not to be deprived of a long life against people who, by virtue of their assets (material and cultural), indirectly contribute to the foreshortening of his life chances. There is no legal mechanism for claiming compensation from people who live in Chelsea. That is because no one individual owes him the right to such a long life. Responsibility for picking up the pieces is shifted onto government. It is expected to fulfil people's needs by taxing resources from the population to fund the palliatives that are supposed to mitigate the pain of the social outcasts. That this model is grotesquely imperfect is confirmed by the millions of young people throughout Europe whose right to work is actively denied to them by State-sanctioned policies ("austerity").

What would an effective human right look like? It is a right that can be asserted *against* others. But which others? And on what terms? Why should you, going about your private business, be the guarantor of another person's right to work, or to be adequately housed? You may wish to help a homeless person, out of charitable sympathy; but that is different from an obligation based on his assertion of a right.

On what basis, then, may the boy from Stockton-on-Tees seek to enforce his right to "a standard of living adequate for the health and well-being of [his] family, including food, clothing, housing and medical care and necessary social services"? The right cannot be at the expense of your property. That would be an invasion of your right to exclusive enjoyment of what is yours.

The solution is to be found in the realm of social rights. These rights are realised through the relationships we have with each other in civilised communities. The right is upheld through the public agencies that are mandated to collect and share on an equal basis that stream of value that you, and I – and everyone else – jointly create in the process of fulfilling the needs of our social personalities. That layer of value is not your wages. Nor is it the returns on the value that you save and invest out of your earned income. These belong to you, and no-one has a *right* to any portion of them. You may wish to share your resources on a voluntary and charitable basis, but that has nothing to do with enforcing human rights through the intervention of State agencies. Income that we produce in partnership with each other is another matter. We all have a human right to a share of it in time of need (say, through involuntary unemployment).

The UN/European doctrine of human rights fails because it does not recognise the nuanced nature of the value that we generate by our labours. Value is treated simplistically, as if it is created by the individual. The failure to differentiate what is mine, and what is yours, from what is ours, injures the welfare of everyone. It results in behaviour (such as pollution in all its manifestations) that damages the well-being of communities and the environment. The fatal omission from the doctrine goes under the heading of responsibilities.

A complete doctrine needs to be entitled Bill of Rights and Responsibilities. We all have private and social rights. We all have private and social obligations. When obligations are acknowledged, it becomes possible to articulate the corresponding institutions and processes that enforce private rights. Those rights would become *enforceable* and not, as under the current tax regime, subject to the ideological whims of politicians. In Britain, millions of families understand that their social benefits are not guaranteed; they can be cancelled or amended at the discretion of government.

The current state of affairs rests on a human rights agenda that was conceived as if to serve those who did not wish to be held responsible for the rights which they exercised. Whether intentional or not, that explains the absence of the social component in the doctrine of human rights. Its absence frees individuals and governments to abuse the value which each of us creates in common with others. It frees them to deprive us of our share of the stream of the nation's rents. But would the remedy create a new injustice? If the solution is one of securing everyone's equal right to share in the rents of the kingdom, through a restructured revenue system, would that deprive current owners of their possessions?

Property rights and rites

The AGR doctrine obliges people to pay the full (marginal) cost of the public services which they enjoy. This entails no radical departure from what they do on a daily basis. When they visit a supermarket and fill up their trolley baskets with the goods they want to consume, they do not expect to cover (say) half of the costs of their purchases. *Low income families living in tenanted accommodation already meet this standard of fiscal rectitude.* They pay their taxes, and they pay rents to landlords – the rents being proportionate to the value of the services accessed at the locations where they live. But as we saw in Chapter 6, it is a different story for residential land owners. If they covered the costs of the public services they accessed, where they lived, the capital value of the land would be zero. Their earned incomes would be tax-free, but that would not mollify some rent-seekers. Does this create an insuperable problem? Alfred Marshall, the distinguished Cambridge economist, raised this question when he noted that

' if from the first the State had retained true rents in its own hands, the vigour of industry and accumulation need not have been impaired; and nothing at all like this can be said of the incomes derived from property made by man.' [1]

But the State had not retained the rents. They had been captured by people who were not interested in social justice, or economic efficiency, or the rights of those whose ancestors had been unceremoniously ejected from the commons of England and the clan lands of Scotland. They wrapped their land grabs in the garb of a perverse system of taxation. The outcome is a moral dilemma. Marshall articulated one variant of that problem.

' The sudden appropriation by the State of any incomes from property, the private ownership of which had once been recognized by it, would destroy security and shake the foundations of society.'

Marshall, as it turned out, was not able to sustain this defence of private property in land. In a letter to *The Times* dated 16 November 1909, he endorsed a fiscal charge "on the public value of land". He observed that "to check the appropriation of what is really public property by private persons...I regard it as sound finance".[2]

The privileged rights of land ownership are indefensible on two grounds. First, there is the problem of the current tax system. Because rents are privileged, taxes are levied on wages and profits. This is an invasion of property which the owners earn. And yet, those taxes are not censured for shaking the foundation of society.

The second problem relates to the injustice on which the current land tenure system was constructed. That injustice did not cease at some date in the past. The injustice is actively propagated to this day. The owners of land continue to be enriched by the rents created by others. Those rents are appropriated either directly (as landlords) or indirectly (as transfers from the public purse).

Are people entitled to correct injustices of the past by negotiating a new social contract? The terms of that negotiation are clear: funding public services

---

1 Alfred Marshall (1898), *Principles of Economics*, London: Macmillan, 3rd edn., p.718.
2 The letter is reprinted in John K. Whitaker (Ed.), *The Correspondence of Alfred Marshall Economist, Vol. 3: Towards the Close, 1903-1924*, Cambridge: Cambridge UP, pp. 235-236.

out of rent is *not* appropriation; it is the *restoration* of people's rights, including those of current land owners. For the AGR doctrine obliges the State to cease taking people's earned incomes.

The consequence of failing to apply remedial measures is the unremitting replication of a higher standard of living for some, at the expense of those who are deprived of their rights to a full life. In a society which proclaims itself proud of its human rights record, the rights of millions of people are routinely transgressed through the medium of the financial system. We are left with two choices. Either bite the bullet and mandate the AGR reform, or fall silent about abolishing unemployment and poverty. If we choose not to restructure the way public services are funded, we are left with the politics of containment: of managing as best we can the distortions and damage caused to people's lives.

Funding public services out of rent is not appropriation; it is the restoration of people's rights, including those of current land owners

---

The luxury of being able to choose between the two options is rapidly evaporating, however. The viability of the Welfare State is all but extinguished. Emerging in its place is the Irresponsible State, which is shifting public responsibilities onto the private sector. David Cameron's administration gave formal expression to this transformation through two Acts of Parliament.

▶ Employers were ordered to raise the lowest wage rates, so that government could reduce the cash benefits received by low-income workers.

A responsible government would have instituted reforms to raise productivity and stimulate an organic increase in wages in response to the pressures from a fully employed workforce. Instead, the National Minimum Wage was invented (which did not, in fact, amount to a living wage). Some enterprises could not afford to pay the higher rates. John Lewis, the firm owned by its employees, cut 1,500 "partners", warning that "higher pay depends on better productivity and greater contribution".[3] To circumvent the law, some employers replaced full-time employees with lower-cost contract workers. The number of self-employed workers rose by 224,000 to 4.76m people in the year to September 2016.[4] Other employers reduced the hours worked by employees so that pay packets could show higher wage rates without a penny increase in take-home pay.

---

3 Paul McClean and Jennifer Bissell, "John Lewis and Next see sharp fall in profits", *Financial Times*, Sept.16.
4 Office of National Statistics (2016), *Statistical Bulletin: UK Labour Market*, September 20.

This was the ruse which led 30 toilet cleaners at the offices of HM Revenue & Customs to go on strike.[5]

▶ To ease the pressure on the finances of the State, small firms were ordered to contribute towards the private pensions of employees.

Some entrepreneurs had to evade that cost by not expanding their businesses. The SME sector, consequently, would lose yet more of its potential dynamism.

Measures such as these increase the psycho-social stresses that foreshorten the lives of people who cannot manoeuvre themselves into the privileged caste of rent-seekers. The added layers of tension, both social and personal, stem not from the desire to improve the material living standards of working people. They stem from the ad hoc approach to solving problems in the way society is governed. Piecemeal policies create unintended consequences for the private sector without improving the standards of public administration.

The Irresponsible State is not a sustainable form of politics. If we wish to correct the injustices of the past and prevent the deepening of those injustices in the future, a Bill of Rights and Responsibilities is needed to mandate the organic way out of the financial impasse in which governments find themselves. Under budgetary pressure the quality of public health and education is contracting. This trend will become more intense in the digital age.

Bring on the robots

Digital technology is now forcing problems and choices on the whole world of the kind which, 200 years ago, were confined to the British Isles. In the realm of public policy, the first industrial society was not able to align technological progress with social responsibilities and personal rights. The renewal of those challenges is dramatised by the dangers in the commercial plans being developed by Amazon, the US retail giant. It plans to replace the highways with the skyways. Order a book on-line, and it will be delivered in double-quick time by an unmanned drone.

In 2016, the UK government and the Civil Aviation Authority (CAA) supported Amazon's plan. Research was accelerated into how to overcome the technological barriers to delivering goods to customers without the use of vans and drivers. But the government failed to alert Amazon to one of the costs of this futuristic way of despatching goods. *The skyways are worth a fortune in rents*. If Amazon is not required to pay rent for the use of that scarce resource, it will convert the rents into a further upward twist in its stock market valuation. Fiscal failure suits Amazon and renders delivery drivers redundant. Amazon will:

---

5 Sarah O'Connor (2016), "The striking effects of Britain's pay rise", *Financial Times*, August 2. https://www.ft.com/content/c38d6c9e-589f-11e6-8d05-4eaa66292c32

▶ *pocket* the skyway rents (a cost is turned into a profit)

▶ *pocket* the savings on wages (shrinking the spending power of consumers), and

▶ *pocket* what would otherwise be paid as income tax and National Insurance (imposing further strains on the government's ability to fund public services).

With this financial prospect in the offing, it is little wonder that Amazon is impatient to overcome the practical challenges that remain with drone delivery. Its accountants have worked out that the cost of R&D will be more than covered by the higher "profits" that would be repatriated to its tax-friendly haven outside the UK. The efficiency with which it conducts its financial affairs was illustrated in 2014: Amazon's UK website sold goods worth £5.3bn

---

Box 7:1 **Who owns the rents of the heavens?**

Because the inventors of the new steam engines were not required to pay rent for using the heavens as a dump for their emissions, they were free to pollute while pocketing the rents of one of nature's most valuable services – the capacity to absorb waste. Consequently, the rate of emissions rose to levels that exceeded nature's capacity to absorb human waste without altering habitats and extinguishing whole species.

If, in the 19th century, governments had charged rents for the use of the heavens as a dumping ground, engineers would have been commissioned to invent efficient technologies for recycling the waste - to cut the rental payments. Because this did not happen, the rents of the heavens were capitalised into the value of the land owned by the aristocrats who controlled the coal seams.

Today, airlines use the heavens without paying into the public purse the full cost of the airways. The solution is a market in airport slots.* Airlines should bid against each other for the use of take-off and landing slots (in fact, they already do this via the "grey" market – landing slots are traded between airlines, without paying the skyway rents into the public purse). That is just one way to recover responsibility for the way we relate to nature.

- In the UK, progress is being made in carbon capture and capturing energy from wind and tidal power. This is helping to replace jobs lost in the fossil fuel industry, but public finance policies still do not equalise the costs (and therefore the prices paid by consumers) arising from the need to switch to the green economy.

- Because of the failure of public policy 200 years ago, 56% of the species that occupy the UK land mass are in decline. The State of Nature 2016 report by the Royal Society for the Protection of Birds documents the fate of 165 species: they are considered most likely to go extinct. This tragedy is attributed to dysfunctional forms of land use in agriculture, and climate change in general.

* Keith Boyfield (2003), ed., *A Market in Airport Slots*, London: IEA.

but it paid just £11.9m in tax to UK authorities, while receiving government grants totalling £1.8m.[6] Looking to the future, government should act in the public interest by

▶ *alerting* Amazon to the skyway rents that will be payable when it begins to use the common resource: rents would be treated as a cost of business;

▶ *briefing* Amazon on the fiscal virtues of concurrent cuts to Income Tax, which would leave more purchasing power in the pockets of its customers;

▶ *buying* the time for Amazon drivers to retrain as drone pilots or acquire other skills to equip them for employment in the green economy; and

▶ *easing* into use the new technology on terms that increased productivity without a legacy of unemployment and social discontent.

Productivity, and the net income of the economy, would then be simultaneously increased without the wrecking effects on communities. Amazon's profits would remain competitive while increasing the flow of revenue into the public purse. Employees and investors would be rewarded for their innovation and entrepreneurial spirit. Everyone would be a winner.

If the AGR method of public finance, championed by Adam Smith in 1776, had been deployed at the outset of the Industrial Revolution – with fossil fuel powering the mighty turbines – the world would not now be enduring the existential threat from climate change (see Box 7:1). Because that did not happen then, the nation is saddled with unsustainable levels of sovereign indebtedness. Spending on palliative welfare measures continues by shifting an increasing share of the costs on to future generations.

If Britain and Europe retain their Treadmill Taxes, they will head straight for disaster when house prices peak in 2026. That event would be followed by the depression of 2028. The only way to avoid this outcome is for people to mandate the authority needed to reform taxation. The logic of the reform does not rest on rocket science.

What is mine is mine.
What is yours is yours.
What is ours is ours.

Compliance with those self-evident truths will determine our personal fortunes, and it will determine whether governance is disciplined and answerable to the people. Rule by self-governance – the mark of an authentic democracy – is a simple one: *We should be free to keep what we create, and obliged to pay for the benefits that we receive.*

---

6 http://www.thebookseller.com/news/amazon-uk-sales-53bn-last-year-304947

The coming tax wars

Existential crises threaten our world. Remedial policies are needed to deliver the inclusive prosperity that would serve as the bedrock for global peace. The European Union model does not provide the template. Well-meaning in its intent, the EU turned into a toxic mix of attitudes and policies and is contributing to "the coming tax wars". Through the prism of High Finance we can diagnose the sources of the most pressing dangers. This is also the means for identifying the policies that pack the power to resolve the conflicts which disgrace the idea of humanity.

The immediate threats to world peace, and the major barrier to a new prosperity, stem from two intimately related sources: fiscal policy and "financialisation".

Most policy analysts focus on the way economies are shifting from manufacturing goods to making money through the financial sector. But financialisation is a parasitic activity: a symptom which feeds on the failure to construct a public finance system that would serve everyone's best interests.

One manifestation of the perverse financial system is stalemate in the governance of nations, most visibly in countries like Spain and Greece. Incoherence in the management of the affairs of state nurtures mass discontent, which has created the political space for the return of extremist ideologies. Shortfalls in the funding of health and welfare services, policing, care of the elderly - these are the result of the breakdown in civil administration, the consequence of a "catastrophic public policy failure". The paralysis in political administration is symbolically

represented by the zero rates of interest on money.

Ultimately, responsibility for the political trauma must be traced back to the causes of a failed form of taxation, which were responsible for dissolving the bonds that ought to be sealing relationships between government, corporations and citizens.

• The shortfall of revenue to meet the needs of citizens is sending politicians in search of dangerous distractions. One scapegoat is the tax haven.

The OECD estimates that tax havens deprive governments of anything between $100bn and $240bn a year. Documents stolen from a firm of lawyers (the Panama Papers) revealed the identities of people who concealed their wealth in tax havens. Governments were outraged. In Britain, the Cameron government had been making great play of wanting to terminate what it branded as the corrupt behaviour of people who secreted their assets from the taxman. David Cameron voiced the public anger with tax dodgers. And yet, given its high moral stance, it is odd that the Cameron government was not willing to contemplate the one fiscal policy that would bring tax-dodging to an abrupt end with a single enactment in Parliament.

Tax evasion would be defeated if governments switched from levies on mobile funds to collecting taxable income in the form of annual ground rent. Land cannot be transferred to the Cayman Islands. The net (taxable) income of a corporation is revealed by its real estate, or by its use of natural resources such as the radio spectrum. Where would Apple or Google be without access to a resource that it does not own – the electromagnetic spectrum? They do not pay rent for the use of that resource. A public register of the value of natural and social resources would deliver the transparency needed to discipline the financial behaviour of corporations. Publicly accessible information would also discipline elected politicians, who would become accountable for transgressions in the sphere of public finance.

But instead of charging rents to reshape behaviour, governments have chosen to go down the regulatory route. Working through the OECD, they have created a heavy-handed plan to force compliance with tax policies that are riddled with loopholes. This is guaranteed to create cross-border tensions, as we have now seen in the case of the EU's verdict against Apple.

Australian tax lawyer Terry Dwyer has long warned that disputes over taxes could lead to military conflicts.[1] The decision by the EU to order Apple to pay €13bn to Ireland, on the grounds

that it received unlawful state aid, has created tensions between Europe and the US. America believes that this revenue belongs to the US (payable when Apple repatriates the profits made abroad). The US is threatening retribution.

Tax grabs by cash-strapped governments will now serve the same purpose as the land grabs of the 19th century. Instead of collecting the revenue they need from home producers, they are desperately eyeing taxable income located within other sovereign jurisdictions. Supplementing the fiscally-induced stresses are the dangers surfacing in their traditional terrestrial forms. Flashpoints include

- **China:** home-grown rent-seekers wasted capital and labour on a vast scale (ghost towns litter the landscape).To distract discontent at home, Beijing is toying with military adventures in the Asian theatre.

- **Turkey:** under pressure from the war in Syria, and popular opposition to what has become an authoritarian regime, Ankara is creating diplomatic and military difficulties for the EU.

- **Russia:** she failed to renew the economy after the fall of the USSR. Now, 50% of the budget is funded out of oil rents. With oil prices at record lows, Moscow is once again proving mischievous on Europe's eastern flank.

A new formula for peace is needed. Might fiscal reform be the catalyst for renewal of the European project? Europe could become the beacon of hope for the rest of the world. As for the UK, she is now free to strike out on that path by herself.

---

1 Terry Dwyer (2016), "Tax dodging and the Coming Tax Wars", in *Rent Unmasked* (ed: Fred Harrison), London: Shepheard-Walwyn.

Europe's fatal affair with VAT

Mason Gaffney

As austerity drives Europe deeper into insolvency and loss of competitiveness, the political crisis is coming to a head. Economic stagnation is inextricably associated with the way governments raise revenue. One of the European Union's policies, the Value Added Tax, has inflicted a pernicious and persistent cost on 500 million Europeans. For as the VAT tax-take grew, banks and public exchequers grew mutually dependent, together building a house of cards based on future tax revenues – revenues that VAT does not and cannot provide, even as it chokes off productive commerce and industry and employment opportunities.

In 2014, the 28 members of the European Union used VAT to collect €975,900 million (equal to 7% of GDP). By the time the people of the United Kingdom voted in their Brexit referendum in June 2016, the tax-take was about €1 trillion.

This means that the losses stemming from VAT alone were €1 trillion: that is the sum on top of what was collected. It is the measure of what the nations of Europe could have produced and enjoyed if, instead, their governments had employed the one revenue raiser that does not distort economic behaviour. And yet, economists fail to highlight these distortions as breaches in the dikes guarding Europe from its encroaching sea of troubles.

As a customs union, the EU imposes tariffs which inflict further losses of wealth and welfare. Tariffs, like all taxes based on transactions in the marketplace ("taxable events") have effects similar to VAT, mutatis mutandis.

The excess burden of taxation is a worldwide problem. An ideological collective of economic scholars and statesmen stands idly by while the defences around their communities are systematically eroded. Worse, many rationalize and endorse VAT, supported by the cartel of international agencies and banks that promote 'harmony' in taxing, lending and collecting. Contrary to the stridently expressed views of libertarian commentators, Europe has not reached the limit of its taxable capacity; rather, it needs a better fiscal system and philosophy, with higher tax rates on narrower and less elastic and less dynamic revenue bases.

1

What's the matter
with sales taxation?

I N AUGUST 2011 S&P Global Ratings lowered the credit rating of the U.S. Treasury. We held our breath, thinking this might be the tipping point before a flight from the dollar. Our Congress, deadlocked, quarrelsome and dysfunctional, seemed to deserve it. And yet mobile international capital saw something, spited S&P, and stayed with US Treasury securities. It seems that we must be doing something right, or at least less wrong than other nations. I would not breast-beat about "American Exceptionalism." I deplore our nation's faults, and failure to face them and reform them. I deplore it when some primitive calls it unpatriotic to spotlight our faults: how else can we see and cure them? At the same time it is foolish to preach that we must emulate Europe, when Europe is sliding downhill faster than we, and floundering as it slides.

I build a thesis around a simple, if partial answer: the USA is the only major nation lacking a national-level sales tax (or VAT or GST). At the same time we raise a higher fraction of our combined national, state and local revenues from taxes on property, and income from property, and from bequests of property. The fraction is not just a little higher, but plain to see even without the microscopes of modern theory and econometrics. True, our fraction of revenues raised from property has been trending downwards for half a century, but even so is still many times higher than in Europe, or in most nations of the world.

A major talking point among corporate spokesmen is to contrast the U.S. nominal corporate tax rate with those of other nations, which have recently become lower. Therefore, they say, we must lower ours, to make us "competitive" (today's buzzword). They give the impression that the income tax base is gross income. I will show below that any income tax, personal or corporate, is less depressive, and has less excess burden, than any sales or excise tax or VAT, however "general." That is partly because labour costs are deductible from taxable income. In addition, earlier economists like Musgrave and Domar and Commons and many others showed that deducting capital outlays may lower the effective income tax rate on investing in new capital goods, often to zero and even below. As Anne-Robert Jacques Turgot, an outstanding public servant, economic philosopher and social reformer wrote, even longer ago, investing is "the beneficial and fruitful circulation that animates all the work of society…"

It is true that nominal corporate income-tax rates in the USA have moved recently to the #1 rank among major OPEC nations. That is not, however, because our rates have risen; rather, others have fallen. Italy's rate, for example, has dropped from 52% in 1962 to 27% in 2012, a huge fall of 48%, while Italy replaced the revenues by raising its VAT. If Italy had prospered, it might prove the point urged by corporate lobbyists. However the well-known fact is that Italy has fallen to beggar status in the EU. It is the biggest beggar among the failing "PIIGS" nations.[1] This is the more remarkable considering that European VATs generally are of the "consumption type" that lets one expense investments.

Today, U.S. economists and politicians of left and right are moving toward a pessimal consensus: lowering tax rates on business and rentier incomes is acceptable so long as Congress also closes "loopholes." Hardly anyone says what loopholes, hiding the vital truth that many loopholes, like fast write-off and expensing of investing in creating new capital goods – genuinely "income-creating" spending – are exactly what have made high rates of income taxation tolerable, and compatible with high rates of investing during the mid-20th Century.

Europe generally uses the "consumption-type VAT," meaning that capital outlays are expensible. This may have the effect of exempting the income of capital from the tax, although it is hard to find a comprehensible definition of "capital," and if it includes land it is extremely discriminatory, and in any case favours more durable over less durable capital, and fixed over circulating capital. This, which should be a major issue, is untouched, to my knowledge, in the literature – but will be touched herein.

James Buchanan has enjoyed great success with his new school of "Public Choice," appearing in many texts as the trunk of a new, alternative economics.

'The Public Choice school argues that the best tax is one with the most excess burden. That is because the excess burden will dissuade voters from supporting any taxes at all.'

One of its tenets, turning previous thinking upside down, is that the best tax is one with the most excess burden. That is because the excess burden will dissuade voters from supporting any taxes at all, and thus shrink government down to

---

1 PIIGS = Portugal, Ireland, Italy, Greece, and Spain. While these are mostly Mediterranean, we will see that many Baltic and central continental nations are nearly as troubled.

where it can be "drowned in a bathtub," in Grover Norquist's metaphor. Many deeply- funded new think-tanks undergird dozens of well-paid economists to orate on the same text.

Europe's recent history seems to refute Buchanan's thesis. Europe's welfare states, or most of them, fast outgrow Norquist's little bathtubs, even though financed by growing VATs with their excess burdens. VAT champions uphold it because of what they see as its high capacity to raise revenue, and yet Europe's revenues keep falling as its nations substitute VATs more and more for narrower-based income taxes.

John Stuart Mill in 1848, citing an even earlier finding by John McCullough, showed that a seemingly "general" sales tax would tax capital for turning over, and thus induce investors to favour those capital goods that turn over slowly. In Austrian terms, the tax induces investors to lengthen the Austrian "period of production," and thus distort the "structure of capital" in favour of "high order" capital goods. In Austrian cycle theory, this is a cardinal sin of public policy.

Modern Austrian writers, however, almost to a man, blame the problem entirely on low interest rates enabled by misguided central bankers. Something is missing there, and that something is tax policy.

Here is Mill's proto-Austrian case against a general sales tax:

' ...if there were a tax on all commodities, exactly proportioned to their value, there would ...as Mr. M'Culloch has pointed out, be a 'disturbance' of values ...owing to ...the different durability of the capital employed in different occupations ...in two different occupations ...if a greater proportion of one than of the other is fixed capital, or if that fixed capital is more durable, there will be a less consumption of capital in the year, and less will be required to replace it, so that the profit, if absolutely the same, will form a greater proportion of the annual returns.
To derive from a capital of £1,000 a profit of £100, the one producer may have to sell produce to the value of £1,100, the other only to the value of £500.' [i.e., where capital is less durable, you must sell more gross to get the same net profit.]

' If on these two branches of industry a tax be imposed ...the one commodity must rise in price, or the other must fall, or both: commodities made chiefly by immediate labour must rise in value, as compared with those which are chiefly made by machinery...' [2]

How memorable is Mill's word "disturbance," 150 years before Darth Vader in *Star Wars* sensed a "Disturbance in The Force." In Mill's and M'Culloch's usage, "The Force" is value as determined in a market before or without taxes based on gross sales.

What Mill means by "capital" is clear from his insightful saying, "Capital is kept in existence from age to age not by preservation but by continual reproduction".[3] Mill's "capital" then obviously does not include land. Capital is not a specific concrete good, like a chair in the furniture shop. Rather, it is a quantum of value

---

2 1848, Book V, Chapter IV, pp. 504-05.
3 1848, Book I, Chapter V, para. 18.

that we can, and normally do, keep existing by using the cash from sales to "meet the next payroll," as they say, to replace the chair. It need not be an identical chair, or any chair at all, for capital in this transition is totally fungible in form and location.

Mill hid this light under a bushel, by offering just one example of a small difference, arithmetic only. It was easy to overlook in passing, which is what later standard-brand economists have done. Austrian-School writers, who should see Mill's point so clearly, have mostly skirted tax policy. We should, rather, set this light in a tower on a hilltop as a beacon sending its gleam across the wave to save the foundering ship of state. This paper therefore returns to it below, as a prime example of the excess burden of any kind of sales tax, including VAT.

Then there is The Ramsey Rule. Most standard textbooks and learned papers tell us that a truly general retail sales tax, unlike an excise tax, is neutral as between one commodity and another. A national tax is also neutral between locations, since it is the same in one region as another. Those conditions are never approached in practice, but in the sales-tax canon that merely means reformers should extend the reach of the tax, as the EU does with its push for tax "harmonization" among member nations, meaning in practice that all should follow-the-leader and adopt a VAT at about the same rate. Sales-taxers in the USA keep pushing for ways to override the Commerce Clause in the U.S. Constitution and allow each state to tax imports from other states.

Thus, Buchanan and Flowers wrote "If the tax is uniformly imposed on the sale of all commodities and services, there can be no real shifting of resources from taxed employments to non-taxed employments. The shift in relative prices occasioned by the partial tax cannot occur under a truly general sales tax".[4] Even Harry G. Brown, no fan of sales taxes, wrote "if there is a tax on the production of all commodities and services…there is no advantage in leaving one taxed line for another line which is taxed to the same extent."[5] Earl Rolph and George Break commit to this view.[6] So does Harold Somers, generalizing that a tax on gross sales is the same as a tax on net income.[7]

Bernard Herber[8] and David Hyman[9] chime in cautiously. Charles McLure throws out caution and boldly damns "…the ridiculously unfair and distortionary *de facto* exemption of interstate sales…"[10] [11]

The Ramsey Rule says that sales tax rates, to be allocationally neutral, should not be uniform at all, but inversely proportional to elasticities of supply and demand. I have addressed this issue elsewhere,[12] quoting A.C. Pigou:

---

4 Buchanan & Flowers (1975: 399).
5 Brown (1939: 254).
6 Rolph and Break (1949: 117.
7 Somers (1964: 17, 26, 27).
8 Herber (1967: 254).
9 Hyman (2005: 617-26).
10 McLure (2005).
11 Gaffney (2000 and 2000a) refutes this position.
12 Gaffney (2009: 52-53).

"If there is any commodity for which either the demand or the supply is absolutely inelastic, the formula implies that the rate of tax imposed on every other commodity must be nil, i.e. that the whole of the revenue wanted must be raised on that commodity."[13]

Pigou's reasoning leads straight as a guided missile to levying taxes *exclusively* on the value of land, because its supply is inelastic. Whether Pigou knew what he was saying we may never know, for he was guarded and cautious and indirect and often obscure and coded, like so many academics fearful of witch-hunters. He had reason to be concerned, since even today, long after his death, some are trying to discredit his ideas by alleging he was a Soviet secret agent. His Chapter XIV, "Taxes on the Public Value of Land," does favour such taxes, but is more hedged.

Richard Musgrave avoids the issue by leaving Ramsey completely out of his classic *Theory of Public Finance*. Many, indeed most modern academics square the circle by first citing and then misquoting the Rule. They apply it only to *demand* elasticities, omitting *supply* elasticities, even though these are the more important part of the original rule. Allyn Young started this ball rolling in reviewing Pigou in 1929: "I shall assume that costs are constant. It will be unnecessary, therefore, to take account of elasticity of supply as something apart from elasticity of demand."[14] The notable exception is Joseph Stiglitz. Consistently, Stiglitz often writes sympathetically of taxing land values.[15]

Modern writers deplore the exemption of "services" from the sales tax base. These writers and teachers refer in their contexts only to labour services, ignoring the service flows of land or capital. This is not from ignorance: they know that the "service-flow" of an owner's home has long been included in the National Income and Product Accounts (NIPA) as a form of income, income consumed by the owner-occupant as the real estate yields it. They just blank that out when it comes to taxing services to the "final" consumer.[16] Then there is the well-nourished doctrine that we should tax consumption in order to exempt saving. The writer has refuted this elsewhere,[17] and will only summarize the arguments here.

Basically they are that circulating capital is the life-blood of an economy, and there are four major vampires draining it away. These are

1. public debts
2. equity withdrawal from appreciated lands
3. preferential tax treatment of imputed incomes from durable capital and lands, and
4. the corporation.

---

13 Pigou (1928: 105).
14 Young (1929: 15).
15 Stiglitz (2010).
16 Anderson (1913: 252).
17 Gaffney (2009).

2

Origins of American exceptionalism

B EFORE THE ENLIGHTENMENT, and the Ages of Reason and Benevolent Despotism, Europe raised major revenues from excise taxes like the hated salt tax (*gabelle*), and tariffs, and tolls (like those exacted by the original Robber Barons straddling the Rhine). It built roads with drafted *corvée* and *robot* labour. In England, Thomas Hobbes, a leading influence on the Stuart line of monarchs, had pushed hard for taxes on what he called "consumption" (meaning in practice the products and commerce of the bourgeoisie).[18] Slavery, serfdom, peonage, and indentured labour were common. Prison labour and the galleys were not unknown, and lingered into the 19th Century, as dramatized in *Les Misérables*. Underpaid Religious staffed schools and hospitals, hospices and asylums. As recently as 1930 England used a salt tax as a tool of its imperialism in India, and beat down Gandhi's passively resisting Indians with extreme cruelty that became notorious worldwide. At the same time it was forcing native Africans to labour like slaves by imposing poll taxes. Margaret Thatcher even tried to re-import the poll tax into England itself, which was her downfall.

French King Louis XVI, briefly playing the benevolent despot, in 1774 appointed Turgot his Finance Minister. Turgot was fresh from his triumphs as *Intendant of The Limousin* (Limoges), where he had converted a stagnant into a thriving province. The *Parlement de Paris*, composed of the First Estate (clergy) and the Second Estate (nobles) articulated dominant attitudes in its *Rémonstrance* to Turgot's Six Edicts of 1774.

> ' The personal responsibility of the clergy is to fulfil all the functions relating to education and religion and to aid the unfortunate through alms. The noble devotes his life to the defence of the state and assists the sovereign by providing council. The last class of the nation, which cannot render such distinguished service to the state, fulfils its obligation through taxes, industry and physical labour...'

The Physiocrats wrote and preached, and Turgot the statesman acted for un-taxing commerce and industry and labour, raising revenues from land

---

18 Neither Hobbes nor any later sales-taxer, to my knowledge, has ever defined "consumption" to mean anything but trade in "personal" (movable) property, excluding real estate.

taxation, and coining the slogan *laissez faire* for their philosophy, which gradually advanced throughout Europe. They schooled both Adam Smith and many of the American "Founding Fathers" in their thinking. Obviously, "liberal" then meant something drastically different from "neo-liberal" today.

The students, in practice, got ahead of their teachers. Adam Smith asked why Spain, jump-started with gold pilfered from the New World, lagged in economic progress. He laid it on the Spanish *alcabala* and *cientos*.[19] These were heavy sales taxes, their nominal rates magnified by cascading, that spared the grandees from taxes on their lands while stifling Spanish commerce and industry.[20] They were "broad-based," which modern sales-taxers tout as raising more revenues, but under Philip II with his broad-based alcavala and cientos, Spain declared national bankruptcy three times.

People today associate Adam Smith with international free trade, but Smith actually contains many passages favouring domestic free trade even more than international trade. Here is one wherein he contrasts Great Britain with Spain and France, noting that the *interior* commerce of G.B. is relatively tax free.[21]

' This freedom of interior commerce ...is perhaps one of the principle causes of the prosperity of Great Britain, every great country being necessarily the best and most extensive market for the greater part of the productions of its own industry." [22]

Today, neo-liberals tout "trade" as a basic social good, but they mean just international trade. Look up "commerce" in *The New Palgrave Dictionary of Economics*: it says "see International Trade." States and cities speak of their export industries as their "economic base," ignoring the findings of Jane Jacobs and others about the virtues of import substitution as key to economic development. Neo-liberal free traders like Charles McLure lead the charge to override the Commerce Clause of the U.S. Constitution and allow each American State to tax imports, to help them raise their State sales taxes. "Neo-" pundits hijack old words to mean the opposite of their originals.

In the new USA after 1789 the Federalists under Hamilton first took control, and began levying excise taxes. In 1794 farmers of western Pennsylvania rebelled against a tax on their maize, which they marketed as whisky to cut down on transportation costs. Hamilton, with his Napoleonic ambitions, led Federal troops to put down this uprising. The voters, when they found him dominating the subsequent cabinet of John Adams,[23] and leading the country into the depression of 1798, retired his party and installed Jefferson, whose Virginia dynasty shaped the nation for the next 36 years.[24]

---

19 Smith (1776: 850-51); Groves (1946: 307, n.14).
20 Klein (1920).
21 "Relatively" is a necessary word. Godwin the idealist 20 years later deplored the growth of taxes on "consumption" (read retail trade). The glass that Smith saw as half full, Godwin saw as half empty.
22 Smith, Wealth of Nations (1776: 851-52).
23 Hamilton was not a formal member of Adams' Cabinet, but dominated it anyway.
24 President J.Q. Adams, 1825-29, had left the Federalists in 1807, supported Madison for President, and been Monroe's Sec. of State. Jackson and Polk were Tennesseans who led Jefferson's old Party against the Whigs.

These Virginians knew their Physiocracy. Jefferson, Madison and Monroe had all represented the colonies or the USA in Paris, as had their friend Franklin, where they hobnobbed with philosophers and picked up their ideas.[25] They were pro-French, even as France shifted from monarchy to Directory to Empire to The Bourgeois King Louis Philippe, 1832-48. It was Monroe who had led the fight for the Commerce Clause, freeing internal trade from excise taxes;[26] Jefferson who wrote the Northwest Ordinance dividing public lands for privatization in small parcels, and bought Louisiana, and brought the Physiocrats Gallatin and DuPont into his circle, and welcomed Tom Paine back from France, and extended easy credit to small buyers of western lands. It was Madison, with all his faults, who masterminded the Constitution, and then, in the War of 1812, used the Federal power to tax property, a power he had so carefully circumscribed.[27] They got the new nation off to a flying start.

The Confederate states, even though fighting to survive, stood on their states' rights against their own C.S.A. government, and bucked an attempted C.S.A. property tax.[28] Jefferson Davis had to finance secession with excise taxes. So Davis put a 10% tax on all farm production, paid in kind – a crushing burden on marginal farmers. Winn Parish, LA, for example, home of Huey Long, in 1863 petitioned General Grant to save them from this "oppression".[29] The C.S.A. repudiated its bonds and currency, and lost the war catastrophically. Following attempted Reconstruction, however, came Hayes, Reunion and Restoration of the old ruling class which ever since, first as Democrats and now as Republicans, has saddled the old Confederate States with the most regressive tax systems in the nation, featuring heavy reliance on sales taxes.

Through the complex turmoil of 19th century Europe the *bourgeoisie* joined the first two estates in the ruling class. In the transition, Louis Philippe of France, reigning between the revolts of 1830 and 1848, earned the title of "the bourgeois king," indicating he did not view commerce and industry simply as geese to be plucked, as in the overworked phrase from Louis XIV'S finance minister Colbert. "The sales tax existed ... intermittently, in various European countries to about 1800, but in the 19th century it played no part in the fiscal development of the important nations".[30] Rulers in several nations, including the USA, fostered *la petite propriété* (in Russia, "kulaks"[31]) as a political buffer for *la grande propriété*. (In Germany, *Grossgrundeigentum*.) Tax regimes evolved with shifting class voting power, in a complex history with details beyond the scope here.[32]

25 Bigelow (1868: IV:195); Van Doren (1938: 372); Foner (1948: 15, 24-39).
26 Norton (1941: 51).
27 Medina (1960).
28 Foner (1988: 15).
29 Brinkley (1982: 11); T. Harry Williams (1969: xii).
30 Shoup and Haimoff (1934: 811); National Industrial Conference Board (1929: 163-66).
31 Originally "kulak" meant any peasant more acquisitive than average, following the Stolypin reforms. During the liquidation phase under Stalin it evolved to mean almost any peasant who opposed collectivization.
32 Wikipedia's anonymous article on Turgot cites many sources on his being followed by many of the best-known economists of the 19th Century.

By the end of World War 2, tax structures in Europe were a mélange, short of anything ideal but not as regressive as under *l'ancien régime*. We will pick up the story later in 1954, when the first VAT began the march back to the fiscal ideals of *Le Rémonstrance*.

Taxation in the colonies

American colonies had little need of taxes, by modern standards. There was no national government to support. French and Indian wars were a major expense, but Imperial Britain paid for much of that to fend off their French rivals. Armed settlers and hunters and vigilantes dealt with most kinds of local crime; volunteers fought fires. Church and extended families covered much of what today we call social welfare and education, such as they were. Companies chartered in England sought dividends in various ways, as from road tolls and by selling off or renting out lands granted them by the Crown. Plymouth Plantation meted out lands to each settler, "and him that had a better (location) allowed something to him that had a worse, as ye valuation wente"[33] – that is, in their crude way, they taxed land *ad valorem*, as many migrants did as they moved west.

Nationwide, when George III's treasury sought to charge the colonies for providing their common defence it was by an excise tax like that on tea. The new nation was born in revolt against The East India Company's monopoly and these kinds of taxes that accompanied it. Tax revolt and trust-busting were built into our very DNA, at birth.

Many of America's "Founding Fathers" visited France as diplomats, and learned from Turgot. Some noted American visitors included Franklin, Jefferson, Paine, Madison, Monroe, Adams, and others. America's revolution against England meant friendship with France and Frenchmen, including liberals like La Fayette, du Pont, and Gallatin. Turgot tried but failed to reform France in his day, but he was one of our Founding Fathers, in the mind. The Commerce Clause of the U.S. Constitution did for the new USA what Turgot had tried to do for France, it guaranteed free trade among the states.

Turgot first made his mark as Royally-appointed Intendant of Limoges (1761-74). There he abolished the mandatory corvée (roadwork in lieu of taxation). He improved roads by other means, like taxing the lands they served. He encouraged

---

33 "Then they agreed that every person or share should have 20 acers of land devided unto them ... and they (who were) appoynted were to begin first on ye one side of ye towne, & how farr to goe; and then on ye other side in like manner; and so to devid it by lotte; and appointed sundrie by name to doe it, and tyed them to certainrruls to proceed by; as that they should only lay out settable or tillable land, at least such of it as should butt on ye water side ...and pass by ye reste as refuse or comune ...And they were first to agree of ye goodnes and fitnes of it before ye lott was drawne ...whose lottssoever should fall next ye towne ...or most convenint for nearness they should take to them a neighbor or tow ...and should suffer them to plant corne with them for 4 years ...*ye rest were valued and equalized at an indifferent rate, and so every man kept his owne, and he that had a better allowed something to him that had a worse, as ye valuation wente*" (emphasis mine). Wm. Bradford, 1627, *History of Plymouth Plantation*, from the original ms of Bradford's history *Of Plimoth Plantation*, Book II. Boston: Wright and Potter Printing Company, State Printers (1898: 258-61).

the now-famous porcelain industry, so that Limoges-Turgot is now a block phrase in that region of France. In 1774 the new King Louis XVI, impressed, made Turgot Comptroller-General for all France. Turgot set about removing interprovincial trade barriers, which he perceived as a major barrier to French prosperity. He coined the term *Laissez-faire*.[34] He also set about reforming the tax system, subjecting the previously exempt lands of the 1st and 2nd Estates[35] to forms of property taxation. This was in the spirit of the Age, the Age of Benevolent Despotism and Enlightenment. Enlightenment included Science and Philosophy, which included Physiocracy as taught by Quesnay at Versailles, and practiced by Turgot.

'Turgot abolished the mandatory *corvée*
(roadwork in lieu of taxation). He improved roads
by other means like taxing the lands they serve.'

While Intendant of Limoges he published his *Reflexionssur la Formation et la Distribution des Richesses* (1766). This short, compact work contains much of the essential wisdom that Adam Smith soon was to popularize and expand with *The Wealth of Nations* (1776). Turgot stressed the important roles of capital, and free markets. He favoured letting the market determine interest rates – not from dogma, but from observing the results of John Law's ruination of French banking in 1720. He would combat poverty by relieving the poor of taxes, while raising revenues from taxes on the value of land – including lands traditionally exempt or under-taxed. He correctly observed that taxes based on land values are nearly the only kind that raises revenues without intervening in free markets, twisting and suppressing incentives to produce and invest. By "invest" he meant paying labour to produce new capital, or replace old capital. He emphatically did not mean the zero-sum casino games of buying land, or old capital, or trading shares in existing companies. Smith visited France in 1766 and consulted extensively with Turgot, a man whose practical turn of mind made him a congenial tutor for Smith.

The Commerce Clause, Turgot's contribution to the U.S. Constitution, has preserved interstate tax competition. It created and has preserved our domestic market, the greatest free trade zone in the world, an essential ingredient of American productivity and prosperity. Like Turgot, our Founding Fathers aimed for domestic more than for international free trade. As the USA expanded the "domestic" market swelled to include many times the land area its founders dreamed of.

---

34 *Laissez faire, laissez passer, le monde va de lui-même.* It is French for an ancient Chinese concept from Lao-tse, and has now been hijacked and distorted by the very kinds of people Turgot meant to rebuke.
35 The Clergy and the Hereditary Aristocracy, respectively.

Until 1933, domestic free trade also prevented states from using sales taxes to raise revenue, for fear of interstate competition. It still tends to cap state sales tax rates. That forced states back on the property tax, just as Turgot recommended for France. Without it, it is likely that state sales taxes would rise to 20% or more in short order, as the wholesome fear of interstate competition was stifled.[36]

The U.S. Constitution was a product of The Age of Reason and Enlightenment. Science flowered. Turgot, like Quesnay, admired the work of William Harvey on how blood circulates, with flux and reflux. Turgot simply wrote that investing is "the beneficial and fruitful circulation that animates all the work of society" – thus capturing the basic idea of modern macro-economics, in simpler language than used today.

'America's Founding Fathers aimed for domestic more than for international free trade.'

The U.S. did impose national excise taxes, emphasizing sumptuary ones like Hamilton's tax on whiskey, but the "Whiskey Rebellion" spoke to its unpopularity, and helped Jefferson displace the Federalists. Jefferson doubled our already vast area by buying Louisiana, accelerating a century of raising major revenues from land sales. Jackson even paid off the whole national debt, and went on to distribute surpluses to the States. Many States squandered the funds, but avoided paying the full price by stiffing their European creditors.

Before lands acquired in the Louisiana Purchase were sold out, President James K. Polk acquired more land clear to the Pacific, our "Manifest Destiny" as he called it. The USA became the biggest free trade zone in the world, perhaps in history, and prospered mightily, if erratically and prodigally, with giant-swinging cycles of boom and bust. We tied the parts together with ambitious long rails, but financed them with land grants that spared us from taxes. When the nation annexed lands from France and Spain and Mexico it left the private titles intact, but freed them from the repressive tax systems of those nations. Americans old and new grew accustomed to low domestic national tax rates, over a long period. State and local governments performed most public functions, and lived mainly on property taxes, a kind of tax with no taxable event in its base and thus little, if any, disincentive effects.

Not until 1909 did the U.S. turn to a corporation income tax, spurred by domestic demands for reform and naval and military ambitions. The personal income tax from 1913 was carefully focused by Progressive Congresses on

---

36 Gaffney (2000, 2000a).

property income. There were no state sales taxes of consequence until 1933.[37] Not until 1942 did Congress turn seriously to taxing wage and salary incomes, and withholding the taxes, and even then rates were graduated so steeply that property incomes, being in the top brackets, bore much of the brunt.

Since 1945 the tide has turned sharply back towards taxing labour more and property less, and yet even so America still taxes labour less, and property more, than most other nations. We stand alone as the nation with no national sales tax or facsimile thereof.

'The USA became the biggest free trade zone in the world, perhaps in history, and prospered mightily, if erratically and prodigally, with giant-swinging cycles of boom and bust.'

---

37 Gaffney (2000, 2000a).

3

From Wirtschaftswunder to Common Market to EU and VAT

W E PICK UP THE STORY IN 1948. World War 2 left Germany devastated, but not for lack of money demand or purchasing power. Wartime rationing and price controls, cum monetary stimulus – "suppressed inflation" – had left Germans with piles of cash in Reichsmarks. Ludwig Erhard, minister of finance under Konrad Adenauer, abolished rationing and price controls. He demonetized Hitler's Reichsmarks and replaced them with Deutschemarks as the new legal tender, lowering the effective money supply by 93%. German families lost not just capital goods, but their life savings.[38] They were "ruined," so it seemed. They didn't even have rationing tickets.

To credit (or blame) Erhard alone would be to oversimplify. Kindleberger and Ostrander supply a raft of details - in fact, too many.[39] Squinting between the lines, though, they tell us that Military Governor General Lucius Clay supported an early report by Colm, Dodge and Goldsmith that called for high taxes on "unjust enrichment," and on property and estates, but low taxes on current "taxable events," to stimulate incentives to work and save.[40] It was in the spirit of V-Day, roughly comparable to the Reconstruction Era following our Civil War. Erhard was the German survivor who surfed this wave at its crest. For brevity here, I will simply refer to Erhard's reforms.

Erhard observed that the only rationing tickets Germans needed after the currency reform were the new Deutschemarks, and they would work hard to get them. The same reasoning implies that they would also put their properties to work, if they owned any – and someone did own all the lands of Germany, and the surviving capital as well. A song of the times captured the spirit and attitude that emerged:

---

38 Heller, Walter W. "Tax and Monetary Reform in Occupied Germany." *National Tax Journal* 2, no. 3 (1949: 215– 231); Hirshleifer, Jack W. *Economic Behavior in Adversity*. Chicago: University of Chicago Press, 1987. Klopstock, Fred H. "Monetary Reform in Western Germany." *Journal of Political Economy* 57, no. 4 (1949): 277– 292; Lutz, F. A. "The German Currency Reform and the Revival of the German Economy." *Economica* 16 (May 1949): 122–142; Mendershausen, Horst. "Prices, Money and the Distribution of Goods in Postwar Germany." *American Economic Review* 39 (June 1949): 646–672; Wallich, Henry C. *Mainsprings of the German Revival*. New Haven: Yale University Press, 1955.
39 Kindleberger and Ostrander (2003).
40 Colm, Dodge and Goldsmith (1946: 185).

'Morgen, morgen, lacht uns wieder das Gluck
Gestern, gestern, liegt schon so weit zuruck,
war es auch eine schöne, schöne Zeit.' [41]

What followed is proclaimed as a *Wirtschaftswunder*, but let us not call it a *Wunder* (miracle) for that suggests a supernatural cause and stifles inquiry into real causes. It was unaccustomed *Armut* (poverty) that drove Germans to perform. The first cause of poverty was the obvious: paying taxes to prepare for war, the total war itself, losing it, being bombed, invaded, morally shamed, occupied and plundered. Second, less obvious, was Erhard's repudiating Hitler's Reichsmarks. Economists who sympathize both with Erhard and private property may cover up the contradiction by calling it "currency reform," a "wealth effect" (or income or liquidity effect), but the naked fact is that Erhard's State simply stiffed its creditors, the German people, thus confiscating their private property without compensation. It came from recognizing that incentives come from *Morgen* (tomorrow) and are only dulled by the security and comfort of holding property in the accumulations of *Gestern* (yesterday). Yes, Erhard believed in free markets and incentives; decartelization and Walter Eucken and the Freibourg School were in vogue. Yes, Social Democrats discredited themselves by opposing Erhard, and it is good press to mock them for their doctrinaire myopia. But generations of conservatives since then have spun the story to blank out the positive (*sic*) role of state confiscation of private property.

Few would deny today that the desperate circumstances of the times necessitated radical "currency reform." Now that Erhard's policy is a *fait accompli*, safely in the past, few would deny its spectacular success – it is an outstanding fact of history. But let us learn the economic lesson. Taxes have two opposite kinds of effects. There are the marginal effects, the kinds that Laffer and a thousand anti-taxers preach, the disincentive effects of diluting the rewards of work and enterprise. But there are also the wealth effects such as Erhard's "Miracle" demonstrated.

'The secret of raising revenues without damping incentives is to select kinds of taxes with powerful wealth effects and weak marginal effects.'

Germany's experience suggests that the wealth effects may even be stronger than the marginal effects. Certainly they are if we "play our cards right" and choose wisely among tax alternatives. The secret of raising revenues without damping incentives is to select kinds of taxes with powerful wealth effects and weak marginal effects. Property taxes come close to filling the bill, and even closer if we exempt capital improvements and movable capital (personal property) from

---

41 "Tomorrow, tomorrow, good fortune will laugh for us again/ yesterday, yesterday lies already so far behind/ it was a beautiful, beautiful time."

the tax base. VATs, at the other pole, fit the Laffer model like a glove: strong effects on marginal incentives, and minimal wealth effects.

With the Marshall Plan the USA undertook to help rebuild western Europe and Japan, with great success. "Social Democracy" was the slogan, to enlist proletarians in the common struggle against the Red Menace, which so quickly replaced the fascist menace of wartime. Former belligerents buried the dulled hatchets of nationalism. French leaders like Jean Monnet and Robert Schuman proposed a United States of Europe, to include the old Axis Powers, but not the USSR or its allies. France needed Germany to stop the USSR, and Germany was too big and robust for France to let go its own way again.

Initial steps like the European Coal and Steel Community and European Common Market grew to become the European Union. The 1957 Treaty of Rome created the European Community (EC), aka "The Common Market." In 1990 a commission led by former French Finance Minister Jacques Delors broached a single currency, a step short of political union. French President Francois Mitterand forced the Euro on a reluctant Germany as the price for France's support of German reunification after the Berlin Wall fell in 1989. The Maastricht Treaty of 1992 created the European Union (EU). The EU adopted the Euro. Soon the EU doubled in size, to 27 nations, including eight former members of the Soviet bloc. France as the leader rode high. Germany's size and economic strength has now passed leadership partly to her, now under Chancellor Angela Merkel.

Meantime, by 1954 the tide had started to turn back toward the attitudes of l'ancien régime with its taxes on producers, merchants and buyers. Maurice Lauré, an engineer turned tax-man, got France to adopt VAT "to meet a fiscal crisis" (although such spin accompanies most political moves). VAT had political and administrative attractions, but economically speaking is only a variant form of sales tax. France introduced the first national VAT in 1954 (the same year it lost at Dien Bien Phu). It was not general, but destined to become so. René Coty was the last President of the fractionated 4th Republic, but Lauré's VAT was declared a success.

Charismatic Charles de Gaulle succeeded Coty, founded the 5th Republic, and presided from 1959-69. A fabled hero of *la résistance, Le Grand Charlie* could get what he wanted, and was President in 1963 when a Common Market committee on tax "harmonization" issued the landmark (Fritz) Neumark Report that found the French VAT to be superior to Germany's cascading turnover tax.[42] The Committee agreed to make VAT the basis of tax harmonization within the growing EU. In 1968 France changed its VAT from partial to general.

VAT quickly metastasized around Europe. The EC required member states to adopt VAT to enter the EU. Latin America also went along. In a second push

---

42 Lindholm (1976: xxx).

around 1990, some industrial states like Canada,[43] Australia, Switzerland and Japan came on board too, along with many "developing" economies in Africa and Asia, until today some 140 nations use VAT. They were pushed along by newly empowered international organizations like OECD and the IMF and the World Bank – probably not what their founders had in mind at Bretton Woods in 1944.

The USA has played a schizoid role, worldwide. The Shoup Mission to Japan in 1949 had tried to pioneer VAT there, although in vain.[44] Harry Truman's agent, Joseph Dodge, blocked it.

'USAID has spent huge sums promoting and subsidizing VAT in small nations. Only the USA itself has rejected VAT.'

USAID has spent huge sums promoting and subsidizing VAT in small nations. Only the USA itself has rejected VAT. Evidently there is a chasm between our international representatives, "the best and the brightest," and the voters at home.

By now, almost all nations except the USA have national VATs. Many leading American economists are urging the same for the USA, chiding us for backwardness. Many prominent economists are pushing parallel proposals as well, under names and euphemisms like "the flat tax," "the fair tax," "the people's welfare tax," and so on.

'I advance a thesis that our *lack* of a national VAT is a major source of U.S. fiscal strength vis-à-vis Europe.'

A united Europe with a harmonized tax system and common currency would seem to have realized the fondest dreams of founding fathers Schuman and Monnet. And yet …mobile international capital is seeking security in U.S. Treasuries, in spite of our notorious flirtation with national bankruptcy. Here I advance a thesis that our lack of a national VAT is a major source of U.S. fiscal strength vis-à-vis Europe; and that established standard-brand U.S. economists are seriously derelict in failing to point this out. Austrian-School economists are also derelict by failing to stress how VAT distorts the structure of capital, a topic in which they have special insight and interest.

---

43 Canada, which calls it a General Services Tax (GST), has only dipped a toe in the water, so far, with a national rate of 5%. Its Provinces, however, are huge. Ontario is bigger than many small nations, and Ontario's rate is 8%, for a total of 13%. Ontario also includes services in its tax base.
44 Brownlee (1985).

4

Europe after VAT:
troubles and setbacks

TODAY EUROPE IS STAGGERING. Many of its nations face bankruptcy. Its stronger members and the institutions they dominate seek to impose "austerity" on the resentful weaker members. Banks hold mostly their government's securities, crowding out small businesses that create most jobs. Unemployment rates are breaking records. Tax collections fall ever farther behind the needs, threatening both the governments and their bank-creditors with insolvency. Real estate manias in nations like Spain and Ireland, new to the perils of prosperity, have collapsed, bringing banks down with them.

Unemployment

Unemployment rates across Europe reached catastrophic levels: 10.4% in the Euro area, and 23.3% for youths aged 15-25. Patterns diverged across nations, with the highest youth unemployment rates in Greece (55.6%), Spain (54.2%), Ireland (34.5%), Italy (35.1%) and Portugal (35.1%). Even in France, a pillar of EU, the rate was 27.9%. Sturdy lowland and Baltic nations were not immune: rates in Belgium reached 18.0%, Denmark 14.2%, Finland 18.9%, Luxembourg 18.6%, Sweden 23.4%. Central European Hungary, Poland, and the Czech Republic have high rates, too. Latvia, where wages were so low and jobs so scarce that she lost about 10% of her labour force to emigration, was proclaimed a success story bys Christine LaGarde, Olivier Blanchard and other faces of the establishment.

Debts, Public and Private

The debts of Greece, Italy and Spain made the headlines, but many "stronger" nations also owed more than their revenues could well handle. Greece owes $315 bn. Even Germany, supposedly the EU's economic bulwark, showed signs of stagnation in the 1990s, leading to the sarcastic epithet "The German Disease." Germany's "Miracle" seems slowly to be following an Olsonian pathway from unity and strength-through-defeat to disunity and weakness-through-success. Germany's claimed debt of about $2.1 trillion is rigged downwards by omitting huge pension obligations, estimated to add another $3 trillion to the total. Some banks in greatest danger include Germany's DeutscheBank, biggest in Europe.

'Governments' creditors are mostly banks,
but these in turn are bailed out by the same
governments to whom they lend.'

Governments' creditors are mostly banks, but these in turn are bailed out by the same governments to whom they lend, a spiral winding only downwards until and unless European governments raise tax rates – and find a way to do so without stifling tax bases. The whole structure rests, finally, on tax revenues, lacking which it is just a house of cards. However, most tax bases fall when they are needed most, and the VAT base is falling fastest. As credit ratings fall, required interest rates rise, so debt service rises, deficits rise, and debts keep growing, a disastrous vicious spiral.

Pop Keynesians may see this as a virtue: deficit finance is the way to spend our way out of recessions. That idea from 1936 would seem to have died with the Stagflation of the 1970-79, and again with the deficit-fuelled crash of 2008, but it keeps rising from the ashes of its own self-immolation. The unanswered question now is, "Who will lend when both borrowers and lenders lack the will and the ability?"

How did Europe and its fellow VAT-sters reach this sorry state?

5

Excess burdens from VAT

THE IDEA keeps resurfacing that a sales tax is made neutral by virtue of being "general." Many great economists have refuted it, only to be inundated by floods of lesser voices in mass textbooks.

Retail sales taxes, however "general" or universal in their apparent coverage, tax capital as it turns over. Turnover is measured by the sales/capital ratio, which is highly variable among different firms, products, locations, stages of the cycle – and tax regimes, which economists influence. Sales taxes depress it heavily. This is not a mindless grouch at all taxes, for we need public revenues, and some taxes have positive effects. This is a rifle-shot at sales taxes, of which VAT is one.

To repeat for emphasis, retail sales taxes tax capital for turning over. Turnover means replacement; and replacement sustains demand for labour. Replacement does not just depend on sales, it anticipates them, and thereby generates the consumer incomes that finance them: turnover is the autonomous variable that takes the lead in the otherwise circular and now vicious circle of macro-economics in which employers wait for consumers, while consumers wait for employers to hire them. Turnover is measured by the sales/capital ratio, which is highly variable among different firms, products, locations, stages of the cycle – and tax regimes, which economists influence.

'Turnover is the autonomous variable that takes
the lead in the otherwise circular and now vicious
circle in which employers wait for consumers,
while consumers wait for employers to hire them.'

By taxing turnover, sales taxes shrink their own base. Arthur Laffer discredited this idea by letting his patrons apply it to *all* kinds of taxes; Murray Rothbard mistakenly applied it just to the property tax, the one major tax to which it does *not* apply because it taxes capital and land for standing still, not for turning over. These errors should not blind us to the truth in applying the idea to VAT and the other sales taxes that "shoot anything that moves". In the lingo of public finance, they are contingent on "taxable events."

Many standard textbooks and learned papers tell us that a truly general retail sales tax, unlike an excise tax, is neutral as between one commodity and another. A national tax is also neutral between locations, since it is the same in one region as another. Those conditions are never approached in practice, but in the sales-tax canon that merely means reformers should extend the reach of the tax, as the EU does with its push for tax "harmonization" among member nations.

As already noted, Buchanan and Flowers wrote that "If the (sales) tax is uniformly imposed on the sale of all commodities and services, there can be no real shifting of resources from taxed employments to nontaxed employments. The shift in relative prices occasioned by the partial tax cannot occur under a truly general sales tax".[45] We quoted and cited Harry G. Brown , Earl Rolph and George Break, Harold Somers, Bernard Herber, David Hyman, and Charles McLure to the same effect.

Capital proper, when affixed to land, becomes "real estate," hence exempt by law from sales taxes, for these apply, by law, only to sales of what we call "personal" property (Due, 1963: 287), and which Europeans, more realistically, call movable property. The most durable forms of capital, the kinds that Austrians believe are over-supplied, are affixed to land, hence exempt from sales taxes and VATs.

Many "Neo-con" or "Neo-liberal" writers deplore the exemption of "services" from the sales tax base. These writers and teachers refer in their contexts only to labour services, ignoring the service flows of land or capital. This is not from ignorance: they know that the "service-flow" of an owner's home has long been included in NIPA as a form of income, income consumed by the owner-occupant as the real estate yields it. They just blank that out when it comes to taxing services to the "final" consumer.[46] John Stuart Mill in 1848 looked deeper, in a proto-Austrian way, and pointed out a systemic bias inherent in the tax. I have quoted him above.

Mill hid this light under a bushel, by offering just one example of a small difference, and only in the form of arithmetic. It is easy to overlook in passing, and standard-brand economists have done so. Tragically, so have most Austrian writers, few of whom analyse tax policy. Their strong tendency is to impute the misallocation of capital solely to misguided central bank policies, blanking out other factors like tax policy.

Harold Groves, a clearer expositor than Mill, makes the point in a simple table.[47] "Store A is engaged in a trade which has a very slow turnover, such as the furniture business; Store B is one with a rapid turnover, perhaps a meat shop."

---

45 Buchanan and Flowers (1975: 399).
46 Anderson (2003: 252).
47 Groves (1946: 113).

Tax bias between slow and fast turnover businesses						
	I	II	III	IV	V	VI
STORE	Operating capital	Gross sales	Sales/ Capital	Sales/ Capital	Tax @ 0.5%	Tax/ Capital
A	$30,000	$30,000	1	1	$150	0.5%
B	$2,000	$100,000	50	50	$500	25.0%

The sales tax is based on Column (II). It gathers much more from B, the meat shop, than from A, the furniture store, because of B's higher turnover and greater volume. B's little capital of

$2,000 turns over 50 times and is taxed 50 times a year, while A's $30,000 turns over and is taxed just once. (Groves uses this table for another purpose, but it serves to make Mill's point as well.)

Again, compare a parking lot with a cafeteria. Suppose both to be taxed on gross sales, including services. The inventory of fresh food in the cafeteria is taxed daily, as it sells out and turns over. The payrolls are taxed daily too, for they add to the gross value of sales. The value they add to the purchased stock of food is capital, too: "working capital." Or, if one prefers to ignore capital of life so brief and so small a claim on the final product, the sales tax is simply a tax on labour. The gross sales of parking lots, at the other extreme, include no turnover of capital at all.

More generally, as Dan Sullivan points out, sales taxes penalize high-volume low-mark-up marketing strategies as against their opposite. Lest one turn up his nose at, say, Walmart, its low prices do not reflect low mark-up so much as low labour-service per dollar of inventory. It also provides acres of free parking, a service of land, like other big-box stores. Sullivan also notes that sellers in better locations, say Rodeo Drive, can have higher mark-ups, so sales taxation favours better locations over marginal ones.[48] New businesses with high start-up costs can deduct them from taxable income, but not from gross sales. Clifford Cobb notes that ghettos have many barber shops and beauty parlours but few shops carrying commodities.[49] One could go on through all the Yellow Pages for thousands of more examples.

Illustrations and Analogies

Within each business there are also differences among kinds of capital. In a retail bakery, for example, there are pies and pie-shelves. The pies come and go, perhaps

---

48 Sullivan (n.d.).
49 Cobb (2014).

several times a day; the shelves last for years; the ovens for decades; the buildings even longer; the sites forever. Many a needy widow with hardly any capital has earned her mite by baking, while renting the site, building and hardware. Her sales/capital ratio is high in contrast with that of the landlord, and orbital in contrast to timber-holding corporations like Georgia-Pacific, Weyerhaeuser, Simpson, or the Kenneth Ford family's Roseburg timber companies around Roseburg, OR.

Adam Smith, with his flair for metaphor, made the point by contrasting cargoes in foreign and domestic trade, in an age of wind-powered ocean vessels.

> '[T]he quantity of that labour, which equal capitals are capable of putting in motion, varies extremely according to the diversity of their employment[50] ...A capital... employed in the home-trade will sometimes make twelve operations, or be sent out and returned twelve times, before a capital employed in the foreign trade of consumption has made one...the one will give four and twenty times more encouragement and support to the industry of the country than the other.'[51]

The case is even clearer when we compare two uses competing for the same land. The one with more turnover pays more sales tax per dollar of capital invested. The tax drives away capital that turns over fast, and reallocates the land to capital that turns slower, or to uses requiring less capital, or no capital at all, like the parking lot. As to the lot itself, it never turns over in the relevant sense of wearing out and being replaced. (Owner A may sell land to Owner B, but mere ownership turnover is a zero-sum transaction in the national accounts.)

Curiously, Harry G. Brown, a relentless critic of holding land idle, as well as of taxes with excess burdens, does not connect his two goals in one consistent system.[52] He does not recognize that sales taxes inhibit using land intensively, if at all. His mentor Irving Fisher may have misled him. In Fisher's tax theory, all taxes should fall on consumption, holding land is not consumption, and capital gains are not income at all.[53]

Chemists have a good vocabulary for it. Land in production is like a chemical "catalyst": it facilitates a process without disappearing into the product. Its "quantum of value" remains intact in the land. Working capital is, at the other extreme, like a "reactant": its corpus and its quantum of value go into the product. That means they get sales-taxed with each turnover – the basis of the Mill Effect. Physiologists have a name for it, too: what is metabolism but the turnover of protoplasm in cells? One could elaborate, and find analogies from other sciences, but the point is made, and will be made once more below with Dorfman's essay on hydraulic engineering.

---

50 Smith, Book II Ch. 5, par 1.
51 Smith, Book II Ch. 5, par 27.
52 Brown (1939: 254).
53 Fisher (1937, 1942).

Difficulties, solutions and measures

"Fixed" (durable) capital is a mixed, and therefore instructive story. The corpus of fixed capital as a catalyst does not get sales-taxed, only its income plus a little extra for depreciation get sales-taxed, as Mill wrote. Separating the catalyst from the reactant in fixed or durable capital is a trifle less simple than with working capital, but only marginally so. The basic mathematics of finance tells us exactly how to divide the product between interest, the net income of capital, and depreciation, which corresponds to the recovery or turnover of capital (and is labeled a "Capital Consumption Allowance" (CCA) in NIPA). We only repeat a sliver of the mathematics here, but lenders, mortgagors, bankers, and I.R.S. agents use it every day. So do millions of innumerate consumers who buy on the installment plan, taking the mathematics on faith. Innumerate readers may likewise take on faith the algebra below, but here it is for those who want it.

Let "a" be a level annual cash flow lasting for "n" years. "P" is its Present Value, found by taking the Discounted Cash Flow (DCF) using an interest rate, "i".

$$P = a[1-(1+i)^{-n}]/i \qquad (1)$$

The fraction of "a" that is interest on P is:

$$Pi/a = 1-(1+i)^{-n} \qquad (2)$$

"1" is 100%. The second term as a function of "n" forms a curve of exponential decay (a ski-slope curve) starting from "1" when n=0 and falling to zero when n=∞.

Thus when n=0 the cash flow is all capital recovery – there is no interest income – and the sales tax is based entirely on turnover of pre-existing capital. At the other extreme, when n grows big, $(1+i)^{-n} \rightarrow 0$ and there is little capital recovery, and that little is not taxed until after "n" years. So much for the algebra.

A unit or "quantum" of fixed capital embodied and frozen into, say, the Oroville Dam and the long aqueducts it feeds, or the English-French "Chunnel," or the even longer tunnel from Sakhalin to Hokkaido, or grading steep building sites, or land-fill in shallow water, or The Pyramids, or The Mackinac Bridge, or the marble cladding of Nelson Rockefeller's Parthenon in Albany, turns over so slowly that its net product or service after O&M (Operation and Maintenance) is mostly pure income. That product or service as a tax base, however we measure it, includes little recovery of capital. Too often, indeed, there is none at all, thanks to engineering megalomania coupled with the "irrational exuberance" of land speculators and "earmarking" politicians who trade subsidies for campaign contributions.

As to land, this never turns over. Its ownership may turn over many times, but that is an entirely different meaning of "turnover": it is a zero-sum game, macro-economically. It entails no depreciation and ultimate replacement of the lot, and no routine recovery of the original purchase price through a CCA (Capital Consumption Allowance). In a rational market, land is priced so high that its cash flow is just enough to cover interest on its price, with nothing left over for a CCA. In a rising but still rational market, indeed, interest on the price is greater than cash flow by an amount equal to annual appreciation. In a market with "irrational exuberance," which comes along in a regular cycle of 18 years or so, interest often exceeds the sum of cash flow and appreciation, as we learned so well in 1990, promptly forgot, and went through again in 2008, and began a new cycle of forgetting in 2013.

Many economists disregard The Mill Effect by assuming, too blithely, that sales taxes are all shifted forward to "consumers". Even if that were 100% true it would certainly depress demand for the over-taxed items. Most economists today share some, at least, of the paradigm of Buchanan and Flowers wherein sales taxes are shifted backwards to factors of production. There is a hint of this in Mill,[54] but the stronger recent statement is in Harry G. Brown.[55] Earl Rolph, crediting Brown, agrees.[56] Richard Musgrave, crediting both Brown and Rolph, endorses this approach in the main, too.[57] Many of us now hew to the Physiocratic doctrine that All Taxes Come Out of Rents (ATCOR). Either way, sales taxes create "A disturbance in The Force" – a massive and basic disturbance. To fuss over trivia, while missing the Mill Effect, would be to strain at gnats while swallowing a camel. For examples of such straining see Shoup and Haimoff, Somers, Rolph/ Break, and almost any popular text on public finance.

Many texts on public finance compare a retail sales tax favourably with a "turnover tax," since the latter taxes every transaction up to and including the retail stage. Thus they dispose of "turnover" by giving it an entirely different meaning than that used by Mill, and used here. They criticize a "turnover tax" (as sometimes used in Germany, and in the former Soviet Union, and now in Ohio) for taxing the same capital several times, "in cascade," as it moves from owner to owner in successive transactions through the "stages" of production. They then criticize how firms may avoid it by integrating vertically. Fair enough, but then they dust off their hands as though done, leaving us the retail sales tax, imposed at only one "stage" of production, as though it were free of taxing turnover.[58] Thus they purge The Mill Effect, the "Disturbance in The Force," from modern fiscal economics.

---

54 (Bk V, Chap 5: 517).
55 Brown (1939).
56 Rolph (1952).
57 Musgrave (1953: 318; 1959: 379).
58 While they are at it, Buchanan and Flowers want to tax unemployed people for "consuming leisure," The euphemism dates from Chicago's Henry Simons (1938). Buchanan and Flowers do not call this a poll tax, for they disapprove of "emotive terms." Yet they do not suggest taxing idle or underused land or capital for taking leisure.

Mark Skousen presents a long valuable list of previous texts and learned writings supporting Austrian capital theory.[59] He argues against policies that drive capital away from "lower order" capital goods that turn over quickly because they are near to the final consumer. You would therefore expect him to take the lead against retail sales taxes, with their bias against these lower order goods. Instead, Skousen switches to another paradigm and favours sales taxes on the grounds that final consumers bear them, and this exempts saving and capital formation. I have refuted this belief elsewhere,[60] and will not repeat the reasoning here.

As to the structure of production, Skousen writes that "a consumption tax… would be highly favourable toward the earlier stages of production…"[61] But "earlier stages of production" means unripe capital, at farthest remove from final consumers, capital that ripens and turns over slowly, the kind that Austrian theory tells us to treat less favourably, or at least *not* favourably. I will not labour the obvious contradiction, but simply express dismay that no Austrian economist, to my knowledge, has ever used Austrian-derived paradigms to criticize sales taxes. Skousen also gives priority to repealing the "capital gains tax," evidently believing that it is a tax on capital, as its name misleadingly suggests. Actually, most unearned increments of value come from land. Taxing or un-taxing them has no direct effect on the structure of capital proper. Most real capital depreciates with time. There are some exceptions, like commercial timber and other biological capital that does add value with time. Here, a pure gains tax would indeed contain a small bias in favour of slow turnover, since the tax is deferred until sale.[62] The capital gains tax as we know it in practice, however, is structured to impose higher rates on faster turnovers.

Richard Musgrave does cite the "Swedish Austrian," Wicksell, who published in German on tax policy, and with great insight. In laboured prose, Musgrave finally concludes that a tax on "gross receipts…leads to a lengthening of the average period of investment".[63]

As to definitions and measurement, some economists see nothing but insoluble problems in measuring or even conceiving of the lifetime of a simple capital item, and even worse problems with the average lifetime of a collection of heterogeneous items. The matter may be made to seem hopelessly complex, and a battery of economists, following J.B. Clark and Frank Knight, ever stand too ready to oblige.

Fred Foldvary, an "Austrian" thinker, neatly solves the problem by distinguishing concrete items of capital as "capital goods," while "capital" standing alone means the quantum of value.[64] This quantum of value is relayed from one concrete capital good to another with each turnover (cycle of liquidation and replacement).

---

59 Skousen (1990, Chap. 4, pp. 84-130 et passim).
60 Gaffney (2009).
61 Skousen (1990: 345).
62 Gaffney (1957: 1970-71, 2006; Vickrey (1971).
63 Musgrave (1953: 392-99, 396-97).
64 Foldvary (2016).

In this relaying the capital becomes completely fungible in form and composition and location. Fungibility is a concept that most economists grasp and teach, although some resist the idea of capital as a quantum of value – something more obvious to accountants, however, and, as Dorfman showed, to hydraulic engineers.

Hydraulic physics and engineering provide a simple solution, ably expounded by Robert Dorfman in an article I cannot praise too highly.[65] Dorfman whimsically calls it "The Bathtub Theorem," and properly acknowledges Knut Wicksell's priority with his "grape-juice model," although Dorfman's model is more general. Dorfman's bottom line is that the higher the sales/capital ratio, the faster a quantum of value will travel through a fund of capital. More briefly yet, the mean turnover of capital is the sales/capital ratio.[66] For the lady baking pies and selling out daily the annual ratio is 365. For the boreal forester the annual ratio is 1/70. Both figures may be modified slightly for elegant variations on the main point, but the difference of 26,000 times illustrates the Mill Effect so starkly, why bother with more? For doubters and masochists Dorfman provides many equations, but ends them delightfully by saying "It is nice that this elaborate calculation is really unnecessary".[67]

Dorfman does not treat land separately, which is a fault. Neither does he analyse sales taxes and their effects. I have supplied the lack.[68] For now it is enough that we can measure turnover simply, and it varies hugely among sales-taxable items and firms.

Professor William Vickrey contributed a general mathematical model published as an Appendix to my "Tax-induced Slow Turnover of Capital".[69] He showed how "Yield Taxes" (sales taxes on timber harvests) slow down average rotation periods. He equates average tree life with the sales/capital ratio simply by inverting the order of integration – a simple trick for him, a mathematician.[70] It was consistent with his lifelong efforts to tax capital gains as they accrue, following the Haig-Simons definition of income.

Summary

We are left with this. Jobs depend on turnover. Turnover is measured by the sales/capital ratio, which varies hugely among different firms, products, locations, stages of the cycle – and tax regimes. Elected officials control the last, and we as economists try, at least, to influence elected officials. Sales taxes, rampant and rising in our times, depress turnover heavily, and so depress demand for labour – both the number of jobs and their pay rates.

---

65 Dorfman (1959).
66 Dorfman (ibid. p.353).
67 Dorfman (ibid., p. 372).
68 Gaffney (1976, mathematical appendix).
69 Gaffney (1971).
70 Vickrey (1971).

Property taxes have the opposite effect, and so may some aspects of income taxation. We do not here address how both property and income taxes may be modified for the better, although they may and should be. Our main point here is that sales taxes (and their twin, VAT) are among the worst possible choices when the objective is to make jobs and raise pay rates.

The USA, with all its faults, has no national VAT. We do not lack for crusading VATsters. They chide us for being behind Europe. As the EU careens to financial crisis, and derivative political crises, while world capital flees for refuge in the USA, the evidence of history is not speaking well for VAT. Forecasting is perilous, and some see doom ahead for the U.S. dollar, but as of this writing the evidence is against VAT. What Dien Bien Phu did for France's empire, VAT is doing for France's economy, and with it all of Europe's.

'Sales taxes, rampant and rising in our times, depress turnover heavily, and so depress demand for labour – both the number of jobs and their pay rates.'

6

Scholarly origins of and support for VAT

W E HAVE SEEN how Maurice Lauré pioneered VAT in France in 1954, whence it grew with the idea of European Union, before going viral around the world. Lauré was not the first to broach the idea, however. Others had been tilling the seedbed before. Of course, everyone touting a retail sales tax had been conditioning minds for years before, but there were only few who limned out the specific form of VAT.

One was the American economist Thomas S. Adams.[71] Adams was disturbed by the growth of income taxes, especially on "business" (property) incomes, and proposed substituting a national tax on gross sales. His prose was muddy and equivocal, and anyway, Andrew Mellon soon led Congress to lower surtax rates on high incomes, relieving much of rich families' grievances and Adams' case against income taxes.

Another was Wilhelm von Siemens,[72] who saw VAT as a technical improvement to avoid cascading in the German sales tax. Siemens could cite some earlier pamphlets as supports, but they and he were only on the margins of power and there was no follow-up. Soon German governments, saddled with debts and reparations, turned from collecting taxes to printing money, causing one of history's worst hyperinflations.

The high income-tax rates of World War 1 in the USA led to a spate of proposals for a national sales tax, including some from Andrew Mellon, W.R. Hearst, Ogden Mills, and his allegedly liberal friend R.T. Ely. While they never prevailed nationally, their views reinforced a climate of opinion that influenced the many states that rushed in a horde to substitute retail sales taxes for property taxes in the 1930s. Another less obvious factor was the 18th Amendment (Prohibition) which cut deeply into Federal revenues from sumptuary excise taxes on alcohol, forcing more reliance on income taxes, both corporate and personal. The du Pont family subsidized the campaign to repeal the 18th Amendment, a less extreme but more successful move to relieve themselves and their class from income taxes.

71 Adams QJE (August 1921).
72 Von Siemens (1918).

The du Ponts, as major owners of GM, also had an interest in holding down gasoline taxes.[73]

The next tranche of advocates included scholars Irving Fisher, Kaldor, Meade, and Prest. Following World War 2, Carl Shoup of Columbia joined the tranche. General Douglas MacArthur as head of SCAP[74] was in a position to dictate many policies to occupied Japan, and he picked Shoup to head an advisory group on tax policy. Shoup, of professorial and objective mien, was the scion of Paul Shoup, President of the Southern Pacific Railroad and developer of upper class Los Altos in San Mateo County. Shoup came out strongly for a VAT.[75] He was one of the first American economists to push VAT abroad. Like MacArthur, he hoped that his policies applied first in a foreign nation would set an example to be followed in the USA itself, but it did not work out that way, either for him or later Americans working for the IMF, World Bank, OECD, and other international bureaucracies.

More recent champions are Pete Peterson, Harold Somers, Michael Dukakis and his advisor Larry Summers, Cary Brown, James Buchanan, Paul Krugman,[76] G.N. Hatsopolous, James Poterba, Steve Forbes, Rick Perry, Robert Hall and Alvin Rabushka backed by The Hoover Institution, Newt Gingrich, Milton Friedman, Richard Armey, Henry Aaron, Charles McLure, Richard Lindholm, John Due, Raymond Mikesell, Arnold Harberger and many others. The Republican platform of 2012 even included a plank to repeal the 16th Amendment and adopt a national VAT. Centrists scoffed at the extremism, but in our times we have seen how fast, sometimes, extreme becomes mainstream.

The EU as Enforcement Cartel

The European Union has required and spawned its own governing legislatures and bureaucracies in bewildering array, layered on top of existing national bureaucracies. These new agencies take on powers and lives and agenda and academic satrapies of their own, like our own Federal Reserve System. Like most bureaucracies they tend to aggrandize and perpetuate themselves and freeze in place. A major recent shift is evident. Control has shifted from Social Democrats to Conservatives representing bankers and other lenders. A critic describes them as the "giant Goldman-Sachs squid." The metaphor is exaggerated, but a useful mnemonic of where power now lies.

In 1998 the OECD was pressuring errant nations to raise tax rates. It campaigned against tax regimes it stigmatized as "harmful" because they might attract mobile capital.[77] By 2013, raising income taxes was off the table, unthinkable,

---

73 More recently Pierre (Pete) Samuel du Pont IV, ex-Governor of Delaware, has come out against state sales taxes. Times and families change, or perhaps "Pete" is cycling back to his ancestor and namesake, P.S. du Pont the Physiocrat. Otherwise, however, he is prominent in ultra-conservative causes and politics.
74 Supreme Command, Allied Powers.
75 Shoup was overborne by the rival mission of Detroit banker Joseph Dodge, representing Truman, who preferred income taxes modified by fast write-off.
76 It is hard to understand how Krugman, today's leading champion of deficits, in 1989 co-authored *Overconsumption*, a criticism of spending,
77 Report of OECD Committee on Fiscal Affairs (1998), *Harmful Tax Competition, an Emerging Global Issue*

unmentionable, a solecism. The prevailing dogma was that raising tax rates would choke recovery and lower the tax base, as Laffer once warned. The focus was on "austerity," meaning to lower spending on social programs and force down wage rates. Protesters in debtor nations see The Troika and its *appanages* as a hydra-headed cartel of bankers and Germans to reduce them to debt slavery. Conspiracy theory and paranoia? More likely what we see is just the unconscious or semi-conscious comity of people with common interests working in harmony. Either way the results are much the same.

One thing the old and the new EU agencies share in common is making an ideal of tax "uniformity" among nations. Sales-taxers have long seen their need for the same ideal within nations or even big states. California is our biggest State in all but area, and also the most isolated by topography, so it most resembles a nation. Accordingly, it has led the march to state sales taxes. For example, in 1955, California sales-taxers invoked the doctrine of "uniformity": if only every city raised the sales tax, no retailer or buyer could escape it by fleeing to a city without one. Accordingly, our Legislature encouraged local sales taxes state-wide.[78] The State collects it, and returns it to each municipality of origin. A central power can overcome interjurisdictional tax competition, as Europe's Troika agencies are attempting now. Thus, EU was the necessary pre-condition for VAT. The two have grown together.

'Europe now enjoys a colossal Peace Dividend, one of the biggest and longest in history. The idea that this should lead to national bankruptcies is absurd and ridiculous.'

Why do lender groups like Europe's Troika come to the aid of debtors approaching peonage?

It is a survival mechanism found in nature. Most parasites stop short of destroying their hosts because they need them for the future. Most predator populations leave behind a saving remnant of their prey to supply the next generation of their food supply. Mankind most consciously saves both the seed corn and the breeding stock for future generations. Thus lender groups have an interest in keeping borrowers solvent enough to repay the principal of debts, while also risky enough to have low credit ratings calling for high interest rates. Lenders also want to discourage debtors from seeking other lenders, and maintain a united front to discipline debtors who default.

Has Europe reached the limit of its taxable capacity? The thought is nonsense in the light of history. The Cold War wound down from 1989. Today the USA,

---

78 Bradley-Burns Uniform Local Sales Tax Act, Revenue and Taxation Code Section 7200.

the only nation with no VAT, bears the cost of policing and defending Europe, and most of the world too. Europe for centuries before now poured its treasures into a series of internecine wars from which the EU has rescued it. Europe now

---

'The bottom line is that Europe is strangling itself with VAT, while the USA, for all its many serious faults, is surviving better without one.'

---

enjoys a colossal Peace Dividend, one of the biggest and longest in history. The idea that this should lead to national bankruptcies is absurd and ridiculous on its face. The alternative hypothesis is that Europe's woes are endogenous. A major cause is heavy reliance on VAT – the main tax to which Laffer's warnings might apply – and the lack of substantial taxes on property or its income, the taxes to which Laffer's strictures least apply. The evidence of Europe's solvency and untapped taxable capacity is the high level of its land prices compared with America's. International buyers are paying record-smashing figures for homes in world-class neighbourhoods like Woodside and Los Alto Hills, San Mateo County, for example, because our prices, steep as they look to us, are still cheaper and the quality of life may be better than in counterpart regions of Europe.[79]

The bottom line is that Europe is strangling itself with VAT, while the USA, for all its many serious faults, is surviving better without one. Well may we chant, "*Vive la différence!*" We still cling to the remnants of a property tax system inherited from earlier times when we led the world in real production and real *per capita* income, making us a magnet for immigrants from the world – from

---

'Let us pray that the python of VAT never wraps us in its coils; let us work to make that prayer come true.'

---

the "wretched refuse" kind to the most talented kind, both of which strengthen us when we offer them chances to work and invest productively. We have an income tax system that, while riddled now with counterproductive loopholes, still prohibits the tax-depreciation of land and occasionally succeeds in taxing the unearned increment of land values. We still find some investment "loopholes" that were designed constructively to reward real income-creating investing in new capital. Let us pray that the python of VAT never wraps us in its coils; let us work to make that prayer come true.

---

79 LAT 1-29-13, p.B5.

Bibliography

"On saving Europe", *The Economist*, 9-17-2011.

Aaron, Henry, and Harvey Galper, 1985, *Assessing Tax Reform*. Washington: The Brookings Institution Adams, Thomas S., 1921, "Fundamental Problems of Federal Income Taxation". QJE 35 (4):528-53.

Andelson, Robert A., with Mason Gaffney, 1979. "E.R.A. Seligman's Attack on 'The Single Tax'". In Andelson, R.A. (ed.), *Critics of Henry George*. Madison, N.J.: The Fairleigh- Dickinson Univ. Press, pp. 273-92.

Anderson, John E., 2003. *Public Finance*. Boston: Houghton-Mifflin co.

Anderson, B.M., Jr., 1913-14, "'Unearned increments', land taxes, and the building trade" *QJE* XXVIII, pp. 411-14.

Arnott, Richard, and Joseph Stiglitz, 1979. "Aggregate land rents, expenditures on public goods, and city size." *QJE* XCIII(4), November.

Bigelow, John, (ed.) 1868. Autobiography of Benjamin Franklin. Philadelphia: J.B. Lippincott; London: Trübner & Co.

Blommestein, Hans J., *et al.*, 2011. Overview OECD Sovereign Borrowing Outlook, *OECD Journal Financial Market Trends* Vol. 2011 #2.

Bogart, William T., David F. Bradford, and Michael G. Williams, December 1992. "Incidence and allocation effects of a state policy shift: the Florio initiatives in New Jersey". Working paper #4177. Cambridge, MA, NBER. Rpt. NTJ.

Bradford, William, 1627, *History of Plymouth Plantation*, from the original ms of Bradford's history *Of Plimoth Plantation*, Book II. Boston: Wright and Potter Printing Company, State Printers, 1898, pp. 258- 61.

Brinkley, Alan, 1982, *Voices of Protest*. NY: A.A. Knopf.

Brown, Harry G., 1924, rpt 1979. *The Economics of Taxation*. Chicago: Univ. of Chicago Press. Chapter III.

Brown, Harry G., 1939. "The incidence of a general output or general sales tax". *JPE* 47: 254-62. Rpt as corrected in Musgrave, Richard A., and Carl S. Shoup (eds.), 1959, *Readings in the Economics of Taxation*, 1959, Selected by a Committee of the AEA, Homewood IL, Richard D. Irwin, Inc.

Brownlee, W. Elliot, 1985, "Wilson and Financing the Modern State: The Revenue Act of 1916". *Proceedings of the American Philosophical Society* 129 (2), pp. 173-210.

Buchanan, James, and Marilyn R. Flowers, 1975, *The Public finances*. Homewood, IL: Richard D. Irwin Co.,

Chernow, Barbara – see *Columbia Encyclopedia*.

Cobb, Clifford, 2014, letter to the author.

Colm., G., J.M. Dodge and R.W. Goldsmith (1946), *A Plan for the Liquidation of War Finance and the Financial Rehabilitation of Germany*, Office of Military Government For Germany (U.S.), May 20.

Columbia Encyclopedia, The, 5th Ed, 1995 (Barbara A. Chernow and George A. Vallasi (eds.).

Commager, Henry Steele, and Richard Morris, 1975. *The Spirit of seventy-six*. NY: HarperCollins Publishers. Rpt 1995, Da Capo Press ppb.

Commons, John R., 1934, rpb 1961. *Institutional Economics*. Madison: University of Wisconsin Press, 1961; first published by The Macmillan Company, 1934. Vol. II, p. 819.

De Jong, Frank, 2012, Letter to the author, 10-20.

Domar, Evsey D., 1953. "The case for accelerated depreciation". *QJE* XLVII, pp. 493-519.

Domar, Evsey D., and Richard A. Musgrave, 1943-44, "Proportional Income Taxation and Risk-Taking", QJE LVIII (May 1944); rpt in Musgrave, Richard A., and Carl S. Shoup (eds.), 1959, *Readings in the Economics of Taxation*, 1959, Selected by a Committee of the AEA, Homewood IL, Richard D. Irwin, Inc. pp. 493-524.

Dorfman, Robert, 1959, "The Bathtub Theorem". *QJE*.

Due, John, 1963. *Government Finance*. 3rd Ed. Homewood, IL: Richard T. Irwin Co.

Due, John, 1972. "The proposal for a federal VAT to substitute for local property taxes in financing education". *Taxation with Representation*, pp. 41-46.

Ebel, Robert D., 1972, *The Michigan business activities tax*. East Lansing, MI: Board of Trustees of MI State Univ.

Ebel, Robert D. and Papke, James A. 1967. "A closer look at the VAT". *NTA Proceedings*, pp. 158-59 Ebrill, Liam et al., 2001, The Modern VAT. Cited in Kathryn James, q.v.

Ebrill, Liam *et al.*, 2001, *The Modern VAT*. Cited in Kathryn James, q.v.

Eisner, Robert, 1952, "Depreciation allowances, replacement requirements, and growth". *AER* LXVI, pp. 820-52.

European Economic Council, First, Second, and Sixth Council Directives, 1967, 1977, and 2006.

Fisher, Irving, 1937. "Income theory and income taxation in practice". *Econometrica* V pp. 1–56.

Fisher, Irving, 1942. *Constructive income taxation*. NY: Harper and Bros.

Foldvary, Fred E., 2008, "The Gaffney Quantum Leap Effect", *Prosper Australia* htpps://www.prosper.org.au/2008.

Foldvary, Fred E., 2016, "Shifting the Landscape", in Fred Harrison (Ed), *Rent Unmasked.* London: Shepheard-Walwyn (publishers) Ltd., pp. 85-104.

Foner, Eric, 1988. *Reconstruction.* New York: Harper and Row, Publishers.

Foner, Philip, 1948, 1974, Introduction to Thomas Paine, The Age of Reason, Secaucus, NJ: Citadel Press.

Gaffney, Mason, 1962. "Ground rent and the allocation of land among firms". In Miller, Frank (ed.), *Rent Theory.* Univ. of MO Research Bulletin #810, MO A.E.S., pp. 30-39, 74-82.

Gaffney, Mason, 1970. "Adequacy of land as a tax base". In Holland, Daniel (ed.), *The Assessment of land value.* Madison: The U. of Wisconsin Press, pp. 157-212.

Gaffney, Mason, 1988. "Tapping land rents after Prop. 13". *Western Tax Review (annual),* pp. 1-55.

Gaffney, Mason, 1991, '*Capital' Gains and the Future of Free Enterprise.* A paper delivered at a program with James Poterba at the annual meetings of "Common Ground", Philadelphia.; rev. D/91. Used as Working Paper, Dept. of Economics, U.C.R.; and for class notes.

Gaffney, Mason, 1993. *The Taxable capacity of land.* In Patricia Salkin (ed.), *Land Value Taxation.* Albany: The Government Law Center of Albany Law School, pp. 59-82. Also in Proceedings, pp. 60-74.

Gaffney, Mason, 2005. "The sales tax: history of its fallen champions". For class use. Also entitled "Sales tax suicides through history", but lacking long bibliography.

Gaffney, Mason, 2009, "Four Vampires of Capital". *Land and Liberty* , 212 Piccadilly, London, Vol. 116 (4), #1224, pp. 12-17.

Gaffney, Mason, 2009, "The Hidden Taxable Capacity of Land", *International J. of Social Economics,* Vol. 36 #4 , pp. 328-411. Extensive bibliography, pp. 393-403.

Gide, Charles, 1890-91. "The single tax and the *Impot Unique*". *QJE* V,pp. 494-95.

Gide and Rist, 2nd Edn, 1948, *History of Economic Doctrine.* London: George G. Harrap & Co.

Goode, Richard, 1955. "Accelerated depreciation allowances as a stimulus to growth". QJE LXIX pp. 191-221.

Groves, Harold, 1946, *Public Finance.* New York: Henry Holt and Co.

Hagemann, Harald, 2013. "Germany after World War II: Ordoliberalism, the Social Market Economy, and Keynesianism". *History of Economic Thought and Policy,* Issue 1

Harberger, Arnold, 1966. "Let's try the VAT". *Challenge* 15, pp. 16-18.

Hatsopolous, G.N., Paul Krugman, and James Poterba, 1989. *Overconsumption.* Washington, D.C., and Waltham, MA.

Hayek, F.A., 1951. *John Stuart Mill and Harriet Taylor*. Chicago: Univ of Chicago Press.

Heller, Walter W. "Tax and Monetary Reform in Occupied Germany." *National Tax Journal* 2, no. 3 (1949): 215–231.

Herber, Bernard, 1967. *Modern Public Finance*. Homewood, IL: Richard D. Irwin.

Hill, Malcolm, 1999. *Statesman of the Enlightenment – the life of Anne-Robert Turgot*. London: The OTHILA Press.

Hirshleifer, Jack W. *Economic Behavior in Adversity*. Chicago: University of Chicago Press, 1987.

Hotelling, Harold, 1938. "The general welfare in relation to the problems of taxation and of railway and utility rates". *Econometrica* 6: 242-69.

Hutchison A.R., 1968. *Land rent as public revenue in Australia*. Melbourne: Land Values Research Group.

Hyman, David, 1990. *Public Finance*. 3rd Ed. Chicago: Dryden Press.

James, Kathryn, 2011. "Exploring the Origins and Global Rise of VAT". *The VAT Reader*, Tax Analysts 2011, pp. 15-22.

Kaldor, Nicholas, 1955. *An expenditure tax*. London: George Allen and Unwin.

Keen, Michael, and Ben Lockwood, 2007, *The Value-Added Tax: its Causes and Consequences*. (IMF Working Paper 183).

Kindleberger, Charles P., and F. Taylor Ostrander, 2003. "The 1948 Monetary Reform in Western Germany". Chapter 7 in Flandreau, Marc, Carl-Ludwig Holtfrerich, and Harold James (eds.), *International Financial History in the Twentieth Century*, German Historical Society, Washington, D.C., and Cambridge University Press, pp. 169-196.

Klein, Julius, 1920. *The Mesta*. Cambridge: Harvard Univ. Press.

Klopstock, Fred H. "Monetary Reform in Western Germany." *Journal of Political Economy* 57, no. 4 (1949): 277–292.

Lauré, Maurice, 1954. *Influence de la fiscalité sur la formation de l'épargne"*. *Rev. de sciences et legislation financiers*, pp. 290-309.

Lindholm, Richard, 1976, *Value-added Tax and Other Reforms*. Chicago: Nelson-Hall Inc. (Outstanding bibliography included.)

Lindholm, Richard W., 1951. "The impact of accelerated depreciation". *NTJ* IV, pp. 180-86.

Lutz, F. A. "The German Currency Reform and the Revival of the German Economy." *Economica* 16 (May 1949): 122–142.

Marshall, Alfred, 1947. *Principles of economics*. 8th ed. London: Macmillan and Co. Pp. 794- 804.

McLure, Charles, 1972. *VAT: two views*. Washington, D.C.: American Enterprise Inst.

McWilliams, David, 2011. "Small savers will pay price if euro goes into meltdown". *Irish Independent* Nov. 30.

Medina, Harold, 1960. (former judge, Atty. with Swaine, Cravath and Moore, NY). A written legal opinion for P.I. Prentice, of TIME, Inc. Copies on file.

Mendershausen, Horst. "Prices, Money and the Distribution of Goods in Postwar Germany." *American Economic Review* 39 (June 1949): 646–672.

Mill, John Stuart, 1848. *Principles of Political Economy*. People's ed. Boston: Lee and Shepard.

Musgrave, Richard, and Evsey Domar – see Domar.

Musgrave, Richard, 1953, *Theory of Public Finance*. New York: McGraw-Hill National industrial Conference Board, 1929, pp. 163-66).

Nelson, Carl, Gladys Blakey and Roy Blakey, 1935. Sales Taxes. Minneapolis: League of Minnesota Cities.

Neumark, Fritz, 1963. *Neumark report of fiscal and financial committee on tax harmonization in the common market*. Chicago: Commerce Clearing House.

Nevins, Allan, and Henry Steele Commager, rpt 1996, *Pocket History of the U.S.*, Trustees of Columbia University.

New Columbia Encyclopedia (NCE).

Norton, Thomas J., 1941. *The Constitution of the U.S.* Cleveland: The World Publishing Company, p.51

Oakland, William, 1972. "A national VAT". *Taxation with representation*. Pp.61-66.

Oakland, William, 1987, "Value-added Tax", in *The New Palgrave*.

Parlement de Paris, 1784, *Rémonstrance* of the First Two Estates to Turgot's 6 edicts.

Peterson, Pete, 1987. "The Morning After." *The Atlantic Monthly*, October.

Pigou, A.C., 1928. *A Study in Public Finance*. London: Macmillan.

Prest, A.R., 1963. "A VAT coupled with a reduction in taxes on business profits". *British Tax Review*. Pp. 338-41.

Quesnay, François, ca. 1760, rpt 1963, various works.In Ronald Meek (ed.), *The Economics of Physiocracy*. Cambridge: Harvard University Press.

Ramsey, F.P., 1927. "A Contribution to the theory of taxation". *EJ* XXXVII pp. 47-62.

Rolph, Earl, and George Break, 1949, "The Welfare Aspects of Excise Taxes", *JPE* 47(1). Rpt. In Musgrave, Richard, and Carl Shoup, q.v.

Rothbard, Murray, 1997. *The Single Tax: Economic and Moral Implications*. The Mises Institute and London: Edward Elgar. At p. 197. Rebutted by Gaffney, 2009, pp. 328-411, pp. 95-96.

Roy, Joaquin, 2007, *Reflections on the Treaty of Rome and Today's EU*. Coral Gables: Miami European Union Center.

Salmon, Felix, 2011. Europe's disastrous summit. www.reuters.com/us, Dec 9, 2011 00:56 EST.

Sanborn, F. B. (ed.), 1890. *The single tax discussion held at Saratoga Sept. 5, 1890*. Concord, MA, Reported for the American Social Science Assn.

"Saratoga single tax debate", 1890. *J. of Social Science* 27, October.

Schenk, Alan, and Oliver Oldman, 2007, *Value Added Tax: a Comparative Approach*.

Shoup Mission, 1949 and 1950, *Report on Japanese Taxation*. 4 Vols. Tokyo: SCAP.

Shoup, Carl, 1948. "Incidence of the corporate income tax: capital structure and turnover rates". *NTJ* , I, pp. 12-18.

Shoup, Carl, 1956-57, "Theory and background of the VAT". *NTA Proceedings*, pp. 6-20.

Shoup, Carl, 1969, *Public Finance*. Chicago: Aldine.

Shoup, Carl, 1972, "The VAT". *Taxation with representation*. Pp. 67-72.

Shoup, Carl, and Louis Haimoff, 1934. "The Sales Tax". *Columbia Law Review* 34:5 pp. 809-30 and at p.312.

Simon, Herbert, 1943. "Incidence of a tax on urban real estate". *QJE* 57: 398-420.

Skousen, Mark, 1990. *The Structure of production*. NY: The NYU Press.

Skousen, Mark, 2009, 2nd Ed., *The making of modern economics*. Armonk, NY: M.E. Sharpe.

Slitor, Richard E., 1963. "The VAT as an alternative to corporate income tax". *Tax Policy*, Nov.-Dec.

Smith, Adam, 1776, *Wealth of Nations*. 5th Edition. Rpt 1937, NY: Modern Library.

Smith, Dan Throop, 1970. "VAT: the case for". *Harvard Business Review* 48, pp. 77-85.

Somers, Harold, 1964. *The Sales Tax*. Sacramento: Assembly interim committee on revenue and taxation, California Legislature.

Statesman of the Enlightenment – see Hill, Malcolm.

Stiglitz, Joseph, 1977. "The theory of local public goods". In Martin Feldstein and Robert Inman (eds.), *The Economics of Public Services*, International Economic Assn., Vol.43.

Stiglitz, Joseph, 2010, *Freefall*. W.W. Norton.

Sullivan, Clara K., 1965, *The Tax on Value Added*. New York: Columbia University Press.

Sullivan, Dan, 20014, letter to the author.

Surrey, Stanley, 1970. "The VAT: the case against". *Harvard Business Review* 48: pp. 86-94

"Taxation with Representation", 1972, *The VAT: a preliminary analysis*. Arlington, VA.

Tideman, Nicolaus, 1999. "'Better-than-neutral' taxation". Unpublished ms.

Ture, Norman, 1972. VAT: *Two Views*. Washington, D.C.: American Enterprise Inst.

Turgot, A.R.J. – see Hill, Malcolm.

Turgot, A.R. Jacques, 1766, (Kenneth Jupp transl., 1999), *Réflexions sur la Formation et la Distribution des Richesses*. London: Othila Press.

Vallasi, George A. – see *Columbia Encyclopedia*.

Van Doren, Carl, 1938. *Benjamin Franklin*. NY: The Viking Press.

Vickrey, William, 1947. *Agenda for Progressive Taxation*. New York: Ronald Press.

Vickrey, William, 1971. Mathematical appendix to Gaffney, 1971.

Vickrey, William, 1977. "The city as a firm". *Public Economics*, papers of William Vickrey. Rpt In Martin Feldstein and Robert Inman (eds) *The Economics of Public Services*.

von Siemens, C.F., 1921, *Improving the Sales Tax*.

Wallich, Henry C. *Mainsprings of the German Revival*. New Haven: Yale University Press, 1955.

Weiss, Martin, and Larry Edelson, June 18 2012, "Double Trauma Strikes Europe", *Money and Markets*.

Wicksell, Knut, 1901, transl. E. Classen 1938. The "grape-juice model", from *Lectures on Political Economy*. NY: The Macmillan Co., pp. 172 ff.

Williams, T. Harry, 1969, *Huey Long*. NY: A.A. Knopf.

Young, Allyn A., 1929, Review of "A.C. Pigou: a Study in Public Finance". E.J. XXXIX (March 1929). Rpt in Musgrave, Richard A., and Carl S. Shoup (eds.), 1959, *Readings in the Economics of Taxation*, 1959, Selected by a Committee of the AEA. Homewood IL, Richard D. Irwin, Inc. pp. 13-18.

Index

About the authors

Fred Harrison is Executive Director of the Land Research Trust, London. He graduated from the Universities of Oxford and London, and worked as an investigative reporter for a Fleet Street newspaper before turning social reform activist. His recent books include *As Evil Does* (2015), and he edited *Rent Unmasked* (2016), a Festschrift in honour of Mason Gaffney. His blogs appear on www.sharetherents.org.

Mason Gaffney is emeritus professor of economics at the University of California (Riverside). He served previously at the Universities of North Carolina, Missouri, and Wisconsin, and at the think-tanks Resources for the Future, Inc., and the B.C. Institute for Economic Policy Analysis. His many scholarly articles roam across topics covering land and resource economics, macro-economics, tax policy, and capital theory. He retired at age 89, but at 93 remains actively researching and writing. His recent publications are *After the Crash: Designing a Depression-Free Economy* (2009) and *The Mason Gaffney Reader* (2013). Contact: m.gaffney@dslextreme.com

Lightning Source UK Ltd.
Milton Keynes UK
UKOW05f0723111016

284970UK00001B/38/P

9 780995 635104